HORSES

HORSES

Andrea Fitzgerald

CHARTWELL
BOOKS, INC.

Published in 2009 by
CHARTWELL BOOKS, INC.
A division of BOOK SALES, INC.
276 Fifth Avenue
Suite 206
New York
NY 10001
USA

**Copyright © 2009 Regency
House Publishing Limited**
The Red House
84 High Street
Buntingford, Hertfordshire
SG9 9AJ, UK

For all editorial enquiries, please contact
Regency House Publishing at
www.regencyhousepublishing.com

ISBN-13: 978-0-7858-2524-1

ISBN-10: 0-7858-2524-X

Printed in China

Originally published as *The Ultimate Guide to
Horse Breeds*.
All pictures were supplied courtesy of
Kit Houghton, with the exception of that on the
front cover, which is attributed to Flickr Creative
Commons/Terry Shuck.

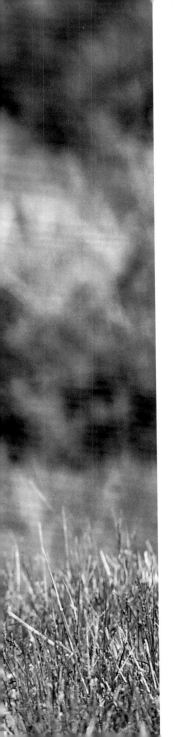

CONTENTS

Chapter One
EVOLUTION OF THE HORSE

THE EARLIEST HORSES

It has taken nearly 60 million years for the horse to evolve from its earliest form, *Hyrocotherium* or *Eohippus*, to *Equus caballus* of the family Equidae, the modern horse as we know it today.

Eohippus (Dawnhorse) can be traced to the Eocene period, between 56 and 34 million years ago, and is thought to have originated in Africa or Asia. Fossils indicate it was the size of a small dog and weighed about 12lbs (5.5kg); instead of having one toe protected by a hoof, as in the modern horse, it had paw pads, with four toes on the front feet and three on the back.

BELOW: A cave painting at Lascaux in the Dordogne, France, clearly shows a horse-like creature. It was painted in around 15000 BC.

OPPOSITE: The Ardennais is one of many heavy coldblooded European horses, probably descended from *Equus caballus sylvaticus*, or the Forest Horse.

Eohippus was a forest dweller, where it browsed among low-growing shrubs and tender leaves, perfectly suited to its environment, its light-brown dappled coat providing excellent camouflage and making it almost invisible to predators.

During the Oligocene period, which began 34 million years ago, Eohippus evolved into Mesohippus and Miohippus, and while still being forest browsers, they were larger, taller and heavier animals. Their teeth had changed from being small and sharp to larger and blunter and therefore their diet. The feet had also changed: there were now three toes on the front feet, the middle one bearing most of the body's weight.

The major evolutionary leap came in the Miocene period, 24 million years ago, when climatic change transformed the once swampy forests into great plains. Parahippus, and eventually Merychippus, now stood firmly on a single toe, the side toes being still retained. Larger than the earlier animals, they now had longer legs which, because they could no longer rely on the cover of trees, enabled them to flee from predators. Like other animals adapted to open spaces, eyes were positioned to the sides of their skulls, allowing them to

scan distances and spot predators more readily.

The next significant development came around 10 million years ago, when the first horses appeared standing on single toes. By now, the side toes had atrophied to what are now known as the splint bones, situated further up the leg. Now known as Pliohippus, though still being rather more smaller and lighter, this was very much more like Equus as we know it today, adapted for cropping grass and for running fast.

The horse made its final leap to Equus during the Pleistocene period,

about 2 million years ago. By now it was perfectly adapted to life on the plains. It was strong, fast and well-muscled and so successful that it quickly spread throughout Asia and Europe and across the Bering Straits into North America.

PRIMITIVE HORSES:
THE THREE BASIC TYPES

It is thought that the primitive horses of Eurasia formed three types, depending upon their habitat and the region in which they lived. The scientific classification given to these horses is

EVOLUTION OF THE HORSE

Equus caballus, which is also the name by which the modern horse is known.

Of the three types, the Forest Horse (*Equus caballus sylvaticus*) was the heaviest in stature and is probably the ancestor of the heavier breeds known throughout Europe. It was ideally suited to the wet marshlands of

Europe, where its thick coat protected it against all weathers and the particularly harsh winters.

The Asiatic Horse (*Equus caballus przewalskii*) was discovered in Mongolia by Nicolai Przewalski around 1881. It is small and tough and capable of surviving harsh conditions. While it is considered an important ancestor of the modern horse, it is distinguished by a slightly different genetic make-up. Although no longer found in the wild, it is still bred in zoos and safari parks.

The third type, the Tarpan (*Equus caballus gomelini*), evolved on the steppes of eastern Europe and western Asia. Well-suited to life on open plains,

OPPOSITE LEFT: The Asiatic Horse (*Equus caballus przewalskii*) was discovered in Mongolia by the explorer Nicolai Przewalski in the late 19th century.

OPPOSITE RIGHT: The Tarpan (*Equus caballus gomelini*) evolved on the steppes of south-eastern Europe and southern Russia. Sadly it is now extinct; however, the Konik, pictured here, is thought to be a distant relative.

RIGHT: The Exmoor is descended from the Celtic or Plateau Pony.

the Tarpan had a lighter build and was faster than the other two types, but like them was capable of withstanding extreme climatic conditions.

DOMESTICATION

The first horses were domesticated in eastern Europe and the Near East about 5,000 years ago. At that time, other animals, such as goats, sheep, cows and dogs had been already successfully domesticated, but it was the need for a larger beast of burden, and one that would produce milk and meat, which led to the domestication of the horse. It was not until later that horses would be used for riding. By 1000 BC, domesticated horses could be found all over Europe, Asia and North Africa. From the original three types

EVOLUTION OF THE HORSE

RIGHT: The Barb, a Type 1 horse, is accustomed to desert conditions.

FAR RIGHT: The Arab is descended from Horse Type 2.

BELOW: The Fjord is a Type 2 pony.

of primeval horse, four types of domesticated equines emerged, two of which could be classified as ponies and two as horses.

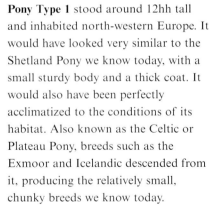

Pony Type 1 stood around 12hh tall and inhabited north-western Europe. It would have looked very similar to the Shetland Pony we know today, with a small sturdy body and a thick coat. It would also have been perfectly acclimatized to the conditions of its habitat. Also known as the Celtic or Plateau Pony, breeds such as the Exmoor and Icelandic descended from it, producing the relatively small, chunky breeds we know today.

Pony Type 2 was somewhat larger, standing about 14.1hh. It evolved in Eurasia and as a result became extremely hardy and resistant to the cold climatic conditions of the region. It was usually dun in colour and had a

could withstand long periods of drought and heat and as a result had a fine coat and a relatively thin skin. It had a longish head, long neck, and a sparse tail and mane. It is a close relative of the old Turkmene horse and also of today's Akhal-Teke. Its bloodline has also found its way into the modern Andalusian and Barb.

Horse Type 2, like the latter type, was predominantly a desert horse, but rather smaller at 12hh. Its home was western Asia and it was hardy and could withstand extreme weather. A horse of great beauty with a fine head and body,

dorsal stripe along its back and stripes on the legs. Prezewalski, Norwegian and Fjord ponies are all descendants of Pony Type 2.

Horse Type 1 was larger than the first two, standing at 14.3hh, and had become adapted to the deserts and steppes of Europe and central Asia. It

ABOVE: The Somalian Wild Ass has the dorsal stripe and zebra markings of primitive species.

RIGHT: Early domestication of the horse in a wall painting from the Tomb of Nebamum, Thebes.
The British Museum, London.

EVOLUTION OF THE HORSE

this was the forefather of today's Arabian horse.

The earliest records describing horses used for riding originated in Persia (Iran) and date from the third millennium BC. By 1580 BC, horses were also ridden in Egypt, and later in Greece. This was a departure as horses had previously been regarded as beasts of burden, riding them having been of secondary importance.

Throughout the centuries, moreover, horse riding began almost to assume the status of an art form, when Xenophon (c.435–354 BC), an historian and military leader famous for leading the retreat of 10,000 mercenaries for 900 miles (1500km), founded equestrianism in Athens: his definitive book on the subject is still highly regarded today.

Increasingly, riding horses came to be used for other purposes, as warhorses or for pulling chariots, tasks for which they had no rivals for centuries. Horses also played an important part in agriculture until they were replaced by

BELOW: Amazons driving a chariot. (Detail from the side of the sarcophagus of the Amazons, Tarquinia, 4th century BC.)
Museo Archeologico, Florence.

OPPOSITE: A Roman mosaic from the 3rd century AD, showing Christ Helios, from the pre-Constantinian necropolis below St. Peter's, in the Vatican, Rome.

steam traction and the internal combustion engine.

Chapter Two
BREEDS, TYPES & COLOURS

Horses and ponies belong to one of two specific groups: breeds and types. A **breed** consists of horses and ponies which are genetically similar and which have been selectively bred to produce consistent characteristics, while reinforcing their best features; they are recognized as such in official stud books. They fall into four distinct categories:

hotbloods, warmbloods, coldbloods and ponies.

Hotbloods are highly strung and include Thoroughbreds and Arabs. They have been bred for their enormous stamina and speed, evident when racing, in which they excel.

Warmbloods are calmer creatures, with heavier builds than hotbloods. They have been bred for their extravagant paces and biddable natures, making them excellent

OPPOSITE LEFT: Hotbloods are bred for their stamina and speed.

OPPOSITE RIGHT: Warmbloods are the product of regional coldbloods bred with hotbloods such as Arabs and Thoroughbreds.

LEFT: The Clydesdale is a coldblood and most are working horses, which means that they are not as universally popular as the other two categories.

BELOW: The hunter is classified as a type in that it has been bred for a specific purpose.

performers at jumping and dressage. They are the result of interbreeding with heavier coldbloods, such as Shires and Cleveland Bays, and were originally bred as warhorses and for lighter work on farms, mainly in northern Europe. Examples are Hanoverians, Dutch Warmbloods and Holsteins.

Coldbloods, as mentioned above, are heavier types of horses and include Irish Drafts and Percherons. They are less common nowadays, heavy horses on farms having become a thing of the past, and are now seen more often in the show ring.

Finally, there is the pony, which covers all the native breeds measuring less than 14.2hh.

A **type**, however, is the result of crossing breeds to produce a specific kind of horse intended for a specific purpose, such as the cob and the hunter.

BREEDS, TYPES & COLOURS

COLOURS

The wild horses that originally roamed the world would have been a dull muddy colour, allowing them to blend in with their surroundings. Nowadays, through selective breeding, horses come in a variety of colours and markings.

Breeding horses to produce certain colours is a complicated business and is achieved by mixing various genetic material. This is a tricky process as some colour genes also have an effect on temperament and performance. For example, the old saying that chestnuts have fiery temperaments often seems to be correct. Racehorse breeders tend to favour horses carrying the black gene, present in the bay, and they do seem to be predominant among the winners of races.

In the United States and Australia, particularly, selective breeding to produce unusual colours has become commonplace, and horses now come in a striking variety of colours and markings. Most horses, however, fit into the basic categories listed in this section.

Bay This is probably the most common colour, the coat varying from a light reddish-brown to deep black-brown with black on the lower legs, muzzle and the tips of the ears, the mane and tail being also black. Bays are a genetically modified form of black. Despite their popularity, only one actual breed has emerged: the Cleveland Bay.

Brown The coat consists of shades of nearly black or brown, which are spread evenly over the body except for the areas around the eyes, the girth, muzzle and flanks, which have a lighter 'mealy' appearance. The mane and tail may be liver, reddish-brown or nearly-black.

Chestnut A red coat of any shade, ranging from a light to a dark reddish-brown which is known as liver chestnut. The mane and tail are usually of a similar colour or may be flaxen (these are called sorrels). Non-chestnut parents may have chestnut foals; if both parents are chestnuts they will always have progeny that are this colour.

Dun There are four variations on the colour known as dun, which can have red, yellow, mouse and blue tinges.

HORSES

OPPOSITE: Colour is determined by genetic inheritance and is often a feature of specific breeds. These wild horses carry a variety of colours in their gene pool.

LEFT: The bay is probably the most common colour, the coat ranging from bright red to almost black.

BELOW FAR LEFT: A brown Barb horse.

BELOW: Chestnuts also come in a large range of colours – from deep liver chestnut to almost golden.

with age, leading to most of them eventually turning white in varying degrees. This is not necessarily a sign of old age and is known as greying out. They come with two different coat patterns, the favourite being dappled grey, which is usually the result of the lightening of the coat of a horse which was born dark grey, known as iron or blue-grey. As the

Dun horses have darker markings on the muzzle and legs, with the addition of a dorsal stripe which may be black or brown. Several breeds of this colour type have been developed, the most common being the Fjord.

Grey Technically, this is not a colour but a pattern superimposed over other colours. Greys are born with dark skin which progressively lightens

OPPOSITE LEFT: Dun is one of the oldest colours, and was probably a feature of prehistoric breeds.

OPPOSITE RIGHT: Grey can range from pure white, as in the Lipizzaner, to a deep almost black colour. This Lusitano is an attractive dappled grey.

RIGHT: The Friesian is exclusively black.

horse's colour fades, the dappling remains mainly on the legs. The other type is known as flea-bitten; these greys never turn completely white, but seem to revert instead to the base colour they had at birth: for example, some may develop blue, black or red speckles; moreover, injuries such as bites and cuts will also grow over in that colour.

Black There are two types: non-fading black, which only fades under extreme conditions, the overall effect being a coat of a metallic, iridescent or bluish shine. When combined with white markings, such as stars or socks, it is particularly striking. Fading black is probably a more common variation: the black colour will only be retained if the horse is kept stabled or rugged when exposed to the elements. There may also be fading through sweating, when lighter patches occur under the saddle and girth areas. When the summer coat comes through, the coat will have a black sheen, but never the blue metallic effect of the non-fading type,

HORSES

OPPOSITE: The spotted gene present in this Appaloosa is a throwback to the prehistoric horses depicted in cave paintings.

BELOW: With its golden coat and pure white mane and tail, the palomino is highly prized: this one is a Quarter Horse.

and during the season will become a reddish-brown in appearance. Black horses aren't popular where the climate is hot, such as in the Australian outback, as black absorbs heat, leading to skin irritation. Breeds selectively bred for their black colour

tend to appear in colder climates, for example, in the Fell and Friesian.

Spotted Spotting can occur in many breeds but is most common in the Appaloosa; in fact, the breed has given its name to the spotted pattern.

also more prone to skin cancers and chafing. In cooler climates, however, they can do rather better, and their striking appearance is certainly unusual.

Roan This comes in a variety of colours and is composed of a pattern of white hairs over a base colour which is only confined to the body, the head and legs remaining in the base colour. Unlike greys, the colour does not fade, but any nicks or

Markings vary from coloured spots on white, white spots on a base colour, or a scattering of small white or coloured spots.

Palomino Much prized, these horses have beautiful golden coats ranging from a pale to a dusky tan; they are usually the result of a cremello crossed with a chestnut. However, the breeding of palominos is a complicated business and is more common in the United States, where

the colour originated. Ideally, the mane and tail should be pure white.

Cremello Sometimes known as pseudo-albinos, these horses have cream-coloured coats which are slightly darker then any white markings that are present. The eyes are pale blue and glassy in appearance. This colour is not popular, particularly in hot climates, where strong sunlight can irritate light-coloured eyes. Such horses are

OPPOSITE LEFT: A strawberry roan.

OPPOSITE RIGHT BELOW: This cremello
Saddlebred is more than striking.

RIGHT: A dramatically marked American
warmblood piebald.

scratches will grow back covered in
the base colour. They come in three
basic types: strawberry roan, which
has a chestnut base coat, blue roan
which has black, and red roan which
has bay. The mane, tail, legs and
muzzle markings will be the same
colour as the base coat.

Coloured The definition of a
coloured horse is any colour
combined with white. In the United
States, these are known as pintos;
however, there is a huge variety of
colours and markings with varying
degrees of white and colour which
have different names. They are highly
prized and their appearance is
extremely striking. In Britain,
coloured types are less popular and
tend to be predominantly ponies,
although horses of the type are now
becoming more common. Varieties
are skewbald, which are coats with
any colour patches with white, and
piebald, which is black-and-white.

Chapter Three
CONFORMATION

When considering the kind of horse you would like to own, be it a Shetland Pony or a Thoroughbred, it is important to understand the rules of conformation which apply to all breeds, in that a horse that is well-made will perform well and is far less likely to become unsound.

Study the horse from a distance and from all angles. It should stand square and the overall impression should be of balance, harmony and symmetry. The head should not be too large and should sit neatly on the neck, which should be gently arched, neither too long nor too short, tapering gradually to slightly sloping shoulders. The legs should be straight and clean with a generous amount of bone below the knee and well-developed joints. Looking at the horse from behind, make sure that the hindlegs are level with the forelegs and that the quarters are even. The buttocks should be well-developed and the tail set high, which is important for impulsion and speed. The chest should be broad and deep to facilitate good heart and lung function.

TAKING A CLOSER LOOK
Now approach the horse. Examine each leg in turn, checking they are perfectly straight and that the hooves are symmetrical with plenty of heel. Make sure they match the size of the horse. (A large horse with small feet will have problems with weight distribution, causing undue pressure to be put on the delicate bones of the foot which could, in turn, lead to disease and lameness.) Likewise, a small horse with proportionately large feet is likely to be clumsy and therefore more prone to injury.

The coat should be bright and glossy and should lie flat; it is a good

OPPOSITE: A horse's ability largely depends on its conformation. This dressage horse has been bred for optimum performance and is therefore near-perfect in its make-up.

RIGHT: From behind, the horse should appear perfectly symmetrical; any crookedness could be an indication of an old injury or a congenital deformity.

BELOW: A horse's legs take a huge amount of punishment and are where good comformation is vital. The joints should be large and the bones straight with strong, hard tendons. The hoof and pastern should form a straight line.

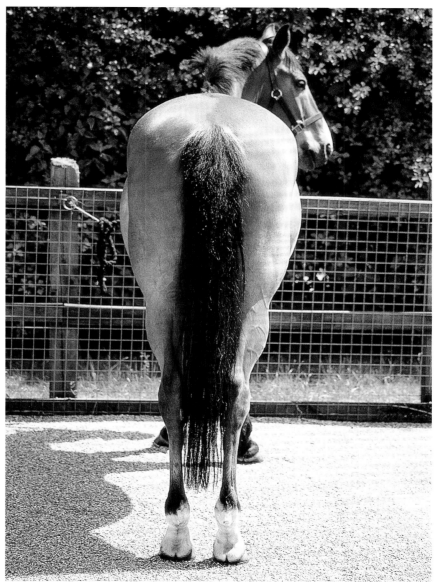

LEFT: The head and neck of this horse sits well on the body. The head should be neither too small nor too large. The eyes should be kind, indicating an amiable disposition.

OPPOSITE: The back takes a huge amount of strain when the horse is being ridden. It should be neither too long nor too short and the straighter the better.

indication of a horse's general health. Look carefully at the head, which will give an indication of the horse's character. The expression should be alert, kind and intelligent, the eyes clear and bright, and with the ears pricked forward. A rolling eye may indicate not only bad temper but also the presence of pain. A 'pig eye', one in which there is a lot of white showing, is said to indicate obstinacy or wilfulness.

Remember, however, that there are exceptions to every rule: often the most unpromising horse turns out to be amazingly talented, proving that first impressions are not necessarily always correct.

COMMON DEFECTS

Legs These, along with the feet, take enormous amounts of punishment during a horse's lifetime. The legs need to be correctly shaped if they are to maintain good action and not succumb to lameness. The knees of the forelegs are responsible for good balance: if, for example, the horse is 'over at the knee' or 'back at the knee', the weight will be unevenly distributed, causing extra strain on localized areas such as the heel. Toes turning in or out are liable to cause strain on the pastern, fetlock and foot. The same rules apply to the hindlegs; hocks which are tucked under the buttocks or which are too far out from the body will hamper propulsion. Cow hocks and bowed hocks are also a sign of weakness and would render a horse undesirable.

The Head and Neck A large head is a disadvantage in the competition field, particularly in dressage and showing. The horse may have difficulty keeping its head in balance, and may find it impossible to hold it in an unsupported outline. A 'ewe neck' is when the top muscle is weaker than the bottom, giving the neck the appearance of being put on upside-down: horses with this defect should be avoided as it is a fault often impossible to correct. Likewise, a bull neck should also be avoided as the horse will be difficult to control and it will be impossible to obtain sufficient flexion when schooling.

The Back This is subject to enormous strain because it has to carry the weight of a rider; it is vital, therefore, that it is as strong as possible. Look for well-developed muscles, which are the major support of the back. The horse's natural conformation is also an important factor: horses with long backs are more likely to suffer from strain; sway (hollow) backs, another

feature of long-backed horses, is another sign of weakness. Horses with short backs have an advantage in that they are usually strong and often agile; however, they are also likely to overreach. It is also difficult to fit them with a saddle and the rider may end up sitting nearer the horse's loins, which are the weakest part of the back.

Chapter Four
HORSE BREEDS

AKHAL-TEKE (Turkmenistan)

The Akhal-Teke of Turkmenistan, a republic in central Asia which lies between the Caspian Sea and Afghanistan, is believed to be a descendant of the Turkoman or Turkmene, an ancient race of horse thought to have existed thousands of years ago, but now unfortunately extinct. It takes its name from a tribe called the Teke which still inhabits the Akhal oasis in the Karakum desert, close to the borders of Iran, where the horses traditionally live in herds under the watchful eyes of mounted herdsmen. This aristocrat of the desert is long, slim elegance personified, but even so has a hardy constitution and can go long periods without water. However, it is usually protected in its native environment when heavy rugs are used to cover its back during extremes of heat and cold. They were once hand-fed a high-protein diet, which surprisingly included eggs and mutton fat.

Historically, this 'heavenly' horse was prized by warlords such as Alexander the Great, Darius the Mede, and Genghis Khan, while Marco Polo praised the Turkoman horse in his *Travels*. Nowadays, because of its great agility and athleticism, the Akhal-Teke is most often used for racing and endurance events.

The Akhal-Teke is independent, free-spirited, and inclined to be wilful. It requires firm but kind and tactful handling and is unsuitable for the inexperienced.

HORSES

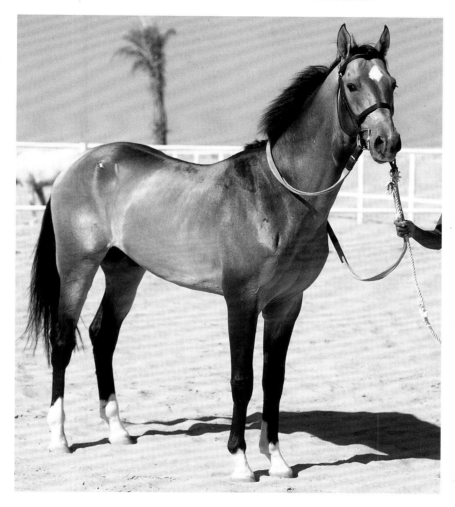

Although the shoulders are broad and sloping, the chest is quite narrow. The body is fairly short, rounded and shallow, and the long loins have little definition. The girth is quite narrow, and the very long legs appear disproportionately long in comparison with the body, and taper to small hooves.

The Akhal-Teke has an unusually smooth-flowing and powerful action. The shape of the pastern is unique to the breed, possibly developed from negotiating sandy desert terrain.

The Akhal-Teke is not known for its sunny nature, in fact, quite the reverse. It is wilful and rebellious and will benefit from one firm handler which it can learn to trust. It is an intelligent animal which requires careful and sympathetic training; it does not respond well to punishment and may well try to retaliate. Due to its genetic inheritance it is unlikely to flourish cooped up in a stable, and must be allowed a predominantly outdoor life, with plenty of space to wander.

Colours are chestnut, bay, grey, palomino, black, dun. All the colours, apart from raven black, are iridescent, which is an extremely striking feature.

It stands at approximately 15.2hh but, with its pronounced withers and high head-carriage, the horse gives the appearance of being somewhat taller.

The Akhal-Teke appears to break almost every rule of good conformation. Its head is carried high on a long, thin neck set at an angle of 45 degrees to the body, giving it a proud, slightly haughty appearance. It has a fine, elegant head with wide cheeks and a straight or slightly dished nose; the large eyes are bold and expressive. The nostrils are dry and flared and the ears shapely and alert.

31

ALTÉR REAL (Portugal)

Portugal has two breeds of horses which are used in the bullring and in *haute école* classical riding – the famous Lusitano (page 172) and the lesser known, but no less noble, Altér Real. The breed had its beginnings in the 18th century, when 300 Andalusian mares, intended for the specific requirements of the Portuguese court in Lisbon, were brought from Jerez in Spain to the royal house of Braganza's stud at Vila de Portel in Portugal. After eight years the stud moved to Altér do Chao, which gave the horse the first part of its name, the second part, *Real*, meaning royal. For many years the breed excelled not only at classical disciplines but also as a quality carriage horse.

The Altér Real breed came into jeopardy during the Napoleonic invasion of 1809–10, when troops stole the best horses from the stud, drastically reducing their numbers. Then King Miguel abdicated in 1832 and much of the stud's land was confiscated.

BELOW: The Altér Real is still much in demand as a classical riding horse and many are still bred in studs all over Portugal.

OPPOSITE: This stallion possesses all the fine characteristics of its Thoroughbred ancestry, particularly evident in the head.

In later years, measures were taken to improve the existing stock by breeding it with Thoroughbreds, Normans and Arabs; this, however, only served to weaken the breed, causing great loss to its original character. In the late 19th century, however, the Spanish Zapata family introduced more Andalusian and Carthusian blood which reversed much of the damage caused by the earlier bad judgement.

The breed finally obtained the protection it deserved in the early 20th century when steps were taken to restore the Altér Real to its former glory. This was achieved with the help of Dr. Ruy d'Andrade who, with two stallions and a handful of mares, founded a top-quality Altér Real stud which he eventually handed over to the Portuguese Ministry of Agriculture which administers the breeding programme today. The Altér Real is still used in *haute école* and general riding.

The breed has all the distinctive Iberian qualities of the Lusitano and

Andalusian, having a fine head with a slightly dished nose, medium-length shapely ears, and a lively, intelligent eye. The neck is short but well-positioned with a pronounced arched crest. The shoulders are sloping and the chest is well-developed. The back is short and strong with large quarters. The legs are hard and very tough, the upper parts being well-muscled with large joints, ending in small but well-shaped hooves.

The Altér Real has a high-stepping action which is most attractive: this, coupled with its strength and power, makes it appear much larger than it actually is. Unlike its Iberian brothers, the Altér Real is not suitable for beginners as it has inherited a fiery and lively temperament from non-Iberian blood added in the early 19th century. It is responsive and learns quickly but needs a competent and experienced rider in order to excel. Usually bay, it stands between 15 and 16hh.

AMERICAN MINIATURE HORSE (U.S.A.)

This is not a pony but a scaled-down version of a horse; consequently it has all the characteristics of the larger animal. The first true miniature horses appeared in Europe in the 1600s, where they were bred as pampered pets for the nobility. Unfortunately, not all miniatures had such a good life and many were used as pit ponies in the coal mines of northern Europe, including the English Midlands. In the 1900s Lady Estella Hope continued the breeding programme, and these are the lines that probably made their way to the United States.

Today the American Miniature Horse is stylish, well-proportioned, and the product of nearly 400 years of selective breeding.

The horses make excellent all-rounders, especially in children's ridden classes, such as showjumping and showing, and are also used for driving. The breed now has a closed stud book managed by the American Miniature Horse Association.

The American Miniature Horse should not exceed 34in (86cm) in height or 9hh. It should have conformation similar to a large, fine-boned horse such as a Thoroughbred or Warmblood. The overall impression should be of well-balanced symmetry, accompanied by strength, agility and alertness; essentially, it should have all the appearance of the perfect horse in miniature.

The horse has a kind, placid and affectionate nature, making it excellent for children and inspiring confidence because it is so easy to mount and willing to be ridden; its small stature also makes it suitable for the less able. The foals are particularly attractive, and range from 16–21in (41–53cm) in height. They may be any colour.

The American Miniature Horse should not be regarded as a pony. It is a true horse in miniature, with all the temperament and appearance of the larger animal.

AMERICAN SADDLEBRED
(U.S.A.)

The American Saddlebred was developed from breeds used for trotting and pacing which were shipped over from Europe, particularly Eire and the British Isles, in the 1600s. Due to their hardy constitutions they thrived in their new home and their extravagant paces proved most popular. It was through these imports that the Narragansett Pacer was developed, named for the bay of the same name on Rhode Island; the popularity of the breed soon spread out along the East Coast.

The Pacer is most unusual in that the feet of one side move one after the other, a trait noticeable in many old breeds originating in Asia and Europe. Moreover, the gait proved far more comfortable than the jolt of the four-time trot. Though now extinct, Narragansett mares were bred with Thoroughbred stallions to produce what was known as the American Horse – an excellent all-rounder – which also retained the ability to learn the pacing gait. These, used in the various breeding programmes combining Morgan, Standardbred and Thoroughbred blood, eventually produced today's Saddlebred.

The American Saddlebred has the inherited ability to move its front and back legs together on each side (known as racking). It is most elegant in motion and comfortable to ride.

Today, they are highly prized in the show ring, equally useful in the harness and ridden classes in which they are mainly used; they are also capable of competing in other events, and make excellent showjumpers and dressage horses.

The Saddlebred is born with a traditional walk, trot and canter but has also inherited the ability to learn the slow-stepping gait and also the rack. However, its high-stepping carriage can be falsely encouraged by keeping the feet long and sometimes by building the feet up; in some cases the muscles under the dock are nicked to produce an unnaturally stiff and high tail carriage (this is illegal in most countries). In other cases it can be fitted with a tail brace when stabled to preserve the high tail-carriage, thus depriving the horse of any comfort when at rest: these practices require extreme modification or preferably banishment if this beautiful horse is to achieve recognition in the broader equestrian world.

The Saddlebred's gaits place it apart from other breeds and include the slow gait or running walk, the stepping pace, and the slow rack. The rack is performed when both hooves on either side are lifted in turn almost similtaneously, and all four hooves are off the ground together at certain moments; this is quite spectacular when combined with the horse's high-stepping action.

The Saddlebred has a commanding presence and subtle expression of movement. The head is small and narrow, carried high, and it has an alert and intelligent expression accentuated by its fine pricked ears. The eyes are gentle but intelligent and the nose is straight with slightly flared nostrils. The neck is long and elegant and is carried high. The withers are also high and run neatly into the back which is fairly long, as is the barrel-shaped body. The shoulders are narrower at the top than the bottom and sloping to create the trademark fluid action. The tail-carriage is naturally high, joined to flat quarters which flow into strong, powerful loins.

The Saddlebred is biddable and easy to train. It is gentle and affectionate, loves people, and enjoys being handled. It is also spirited and proud with a keen intelligence and an alert demeanour. Under saddle, however, it can become somewhat excitable.

Saddlebreds come in all the usual solid colours, including palomino and roan. There is often a good deal of white on the head and legs. The coat, mane and tail are fine and silky in texture. The height is between 15 and 16.1hh.

AMERICAN SHETLAND

(U.S.A.)

As the name suggests, the American Shetland's ancestors were the native ponies of the Shetland Islands, situated off the north coast of Scotland. In 1885, 75 of these ponies were imported to America by Eli Elliot and thrived in spite of the warm, humid conditions of the south-eastern states where they were raised, and where the American Shetland Pony Club was formed in 1888.

Today, the American Shetland is nothing like its Scottish ancestor, being lighter in stature with longer, finer legs. This is because the original American Shetlands were bred with small Arab, Thoroughbred and Hackney breeds, resulting in a small horse rather than a stock pony.

Nowadays the breed excels in various driven classes, such as the two-wheeled roadster, four-wheeled buggy, and light sulky. It is also good with children and

will happily complete in pony as well as breed classes and hunter-pony events. It is ridden in either English or Western tack.

The American Shetland possesses all the showy attributes of its small horse ancestors, combined with the strength and workmanlike character of the Shetland Pony. The head is quite long and is more horse- than pony-like; the nose is straight, the ears longish, and the eyes horse-shaped. It has retained many of the Shetland characteristics, however, the mane and high-set tail being furnished with thick, strong hair. The neck is quite short but the legs could be considered overlong, though they remain strong. The hooves retain the strength and shape of the Shetland Pony's.

Having inherited many of the attributes of the horse, the American Shetland has an equable temperament which, combined with its small size, makes it ideal for children to ride. It is reasonably hardy and therefore easy to maintain.

American Shetlands come in all the usual solid colours, including roan, dun and cream. They stand up to 11.2hh in height.

The American Shetland bears little resemblance to its shaggy Scottish ancestor; infusions of Hackney and Thoroughbred blood have made it more like a horse than a pony.

ANDALUSIAN (Spain)

This is one of the oldest breeds to have been handled and ridden by man: there is further evidence of this fact in cave paintings, which confirm that horses of this kind were present in the Iberian Peninsula in around 5,000 BC.

The Andalusian's lineage stems from the Sorraia Pony, which still exists in Iberia, and the Barb which originated in North Africa, with Arab and Oriental strains. It evolved in the peninsula, most of which was then known as Andalusia, at around the time of the Moorish occupation of 711. The result was a horse with a proud, high, head-carriage, and highly-placed extravagant paces.

It was particularly valued as a warhorse, possessing all the necessary qualities to enable it to perform well in battle. (It is interesting to note that El Cid's mount, Babieca, was an Andalusian.) Later, in the 16th century, the conquistadores brought the horses with them to the Americas where it became the basis of all American breeds.

The Andalusian bloodline is evident in around 80 per cent of modern breeds and has had particular influence on the Connemara, native to Ireland, the Lipizzaner of the Balkans, and the Cleveland Bay and Welsh Cob of the British Isles. This also applies to the American breeds which share direct lineage with the Lusitano, Carthusian, and Altér Real.

But this popularity didn't last for ever, and in around 1700 the Andalusian's

heavy, robust conformation fell out of favour, when lighter, sleeker animals, used for hunting and racing, became more fashionable. The breed suffered even more when a plague and famine almost wiped them out, a few surviving in the Carthusian monasteries of Castello, Jerez and Seville, where breeding continued from the best of the animals.

Today's horse can still be traced back to these lines, the purest and most beautiful of which are still referred to as *caballos Cartujanos.* The extreme rarity of these animals forced the Spanish government to ban their export for over 100 years, but the embargo was lifted in the 1960s, and Andalusians now enjoy popularity around the world.

Today the Andalusian is used for bullfighting and display riding, where its power and agility make it eminently suited to intricate movements. They excel at advanced classical dressage and also at showjumping and are also used for general riding and driving. They are often to be seen in hand in the show ring.

These muscular horses have great presence and beauty. The neck is heavy with a well-developed crest. The mane is abundant and should be kept long. The head-carriage is noble and high, the forehead wide with expressive, medium-length ears. The eyes are dark-brown and gentle, the nostrils flared, and the jaw is large and well-muscled. The withers are well-rounded and the shoulder long and sloping. The chest is broad, the croup rounded, and the low-set tail is thick and

long. The body is rounded and short-coupled, adding to the overall strength. The legs are strong with large joints and the hooves are round and compact.

The Andalusian is famous for its extravagant paces. Movement is elevated and extended, making it look as if it were floating on air. All paces are smooth, showy and spectacular.

Proud, courageous and spirited, but with amiable temperaments, Andalusians have soft mouths that make them extremely obedient when ridden properly.

They have mainly grey or bay coats, but others are accepted by the Andalusian Horse Association. In Spain, according to the studbook, only grey, bay and black are acceptable. They stand between 15–16.2hh.

The Andalusian was originally a prized warhorse, said to have been used by El Cid as well as by Napoleon's armies. It excels in all the difficult manoeuvres of *haute école*, for which it remains famous to this day.

ANGLO-ARAB (U.K.)

The Anglo-Arab derives its name from two of the world's greatest breeds, the Thoroughbred, which is of English (Anglo) origin, and the Arab. Anglo-Arab breeding rules are very strict in the United Kingdom, and only these two breeds can be present. Other countries have their own rules, with some adding elements of their own native breeds, the French Anglo-Arab being one of them. There are other stipulations, however, and at least 25 per cent Arab is the norm.

Because the Anglo-Arab is a mixture of two breeds it is not actually recognized as a breed in its own right, with one exception: the forementioned French Anglo-Arab. There are other variations which appear all over Europe, the Gidrán or Hungarian Anglo-Arab, the Shagya Arab, also from Hungary, the Russian Strelets-Arab, and Spain's Hispano-Arab.

Anglo-Arabs make surperb riding horses and excel in most disciplines, including showjumping, eventing and dressage. They also do well in riding-horse showing classes where their manes and tails can be plaited, unlike the pure Arab which must be left as it is. The combination of the Thoroughbred's complaisant nature and the strength, stamina and intelligence of the Arab make an ideal combination. The interesting thing about breeding Anglo-Arabs is that you never know how they are going to turn out: they can be predominantly Arab or Thoroughbred, or a combination of both; either way they are ideal all-rounders and extremely rewarding to ride.

Ideally, the Anglo-Arab should have the body of a Thoroughbred and the tail and head-carriage of the Arab, although this can vary; some are also lighter boned than others. The head should have the unmistakable Arab traits with a dished or straight profile, though not as extreme as that of the Arab. The eyes show that it can be spirited on occasions; the nostrils are large and flared. The ears are medium-sized, fine, pointed and expressive. The head-carriage is fairly high with a well-developed crest. It should have the good sloping shoulders, deep chest and powerful hindquarters of the Thoroughbred. The tail-carriage can be either high like the Arab or lower as in the Thoroughbred.

Anglo-Arabs are usually affectionate and intelligent. They are also brave and spirited and can be relied on to give of their very best.

They most usually come in brown, bay, chestnut and grey, with black being rare. There is often white on the face and legs but never on the rest of the body. The Anglo-Arab stands at around 14.2–16.1hh.

Anglo-Arabs make great all-rounders, excelling at showjumping, eventing and dressage. Featured opposite is the Anglo-Arab Crocus Jacob, while on the left is the same horse being ridden by Jean-Luc Force of France at the 2000 Olympic Games.

APPALOOSA (U.S.A.)

The gene which produces the spotted coat in horses is an ancient one, as indicated by the Cro-Magnon depictions of such horses in caves. For many centuries horses such as these were highly prized in Europe and Asia and they are often seen featured in 17th-century Chinese art.

The conquistadors introduced the spotted gene to the Americas with stock which they bought with them, then generations of these horses eventually passed to the Nez Percé Native Americans, who inhabited north-east Oregon along the Palouse river. They were probably the first tribe to have selective breeding programmes, and they adhered to strict guidelines to produce the best stock. It was therefore the Nez Percé who first developed the Appaloosa, said to be America's oldest breed.

Settlers eventually wiped out the Nez Percé, however, and the Appaloosa dispersed throughout the country, the strains made weaker through random breeding.

Nowadays the Appaloosa is enjoying renewed popularity: the horse does not have to be spotted but there are three additional requirements: sclera around the eyeball, striped hooves, and the skin beneath the hair must be mottled.

The Appaloosa is an excellent all-rounder, commonly used in Western events such as roping, cow pony and barrel racing, and looks well in Western tack. They also appear in showing classes, particularly in Britain, such as riding horse and coloured horse, and are also good at cross-country and showjumping.

There are some obvious differences between American and European Appaloosas. The U.S. types have been

crossed with Quarter Horses and have developed the size and conformation of this breed. In Europe, Appaloosas are larger and more like warmbloods, making them ideal for jumping and dressage. These are also becoming popular in the United States.

This is a workmanlike horse, the head being fairly plain with short, tapered ears. The eyes are alert and inquisitive with the mandatory white rings or sclera around the edges of the eyeballs. The neck and body are compact and well-muscled and the quarters are powerful with well-developed limbs. The tail and mane hair is usually quite sparse. The hooves should be striped.

Appaloosas are great all-rounders: they are good-natured and hardy with plenty of stamina, speed and agility. They stand between 14.2 and 15.2hh.

Coats come in various colour permutations, including white with chestnut, bay and black. They can also be one overall colour or roan. Variations are as follows:

Blanket White over the quarters and loins with a contrasting base colour.

Spots White or dark spots appearing over all or on a portion of the body.

Blanket with Spots A combination of the above.

Roan Blanket Partially roan, usually patterned over the quarters and loins.

Roan Blanket with Spots A roan blanket which has spots within it.

Leopard White with dark spots.

Snowflake Dominant spotting over the quarters and loins.

Frost White specks with a dark background.

The Appaloosa has long been the popular choice of Native Americans. Today, however, it is enjoying worldwide popularity.

ARABIAN (Middle East)

The Arab, or Arabian, is one of the oldest
of the hotblooded breeds, and its
bloodlines are present in many modern
breeds of today which extend throughout
Europe and the United States. The name
is not strictly accurate as the original
'Arab' could have been a small Oriental-
type wild horse which lived in Eastern
Europe and the Near and Middle East.
The Arab was further developed as Islam
assimilated the breed and Muslim invaders
used it as a cavalry horse. Today's modern
Arabians can date their descent from five
foundation mares known as Al-Khamesh
(The Five), said to have been selected by
Mohammed himself for their obedience.

The Arab was also of great
importance to the Bedouin, the nomadic
Arabs of the desert, who can trace their
association with the breed back to 3000
BC to a mare called Baz and a stallion
called Hoshaba. Arab blood is therefore
highly effective when mixed with other
breeds, and usually brings great
improvements to the resulting offspring.

Arab horses were so-named when
they were imported from the Arabian
peninsula to Britain in the 19th century.
The Arab is also the foundation horse for
the Thoroughbred.

Arabs are extremely beautiful, with a
delicacy that belies their strength and
stamina. They shine in riding events such

as dressage, riding horse, and in-hand showing. They also excel in disciplines that rely on strength, such as endurance riding and racing. Arabs have the reputation of being unable to jump, which is untrue; they are in fact keen jumpers, although lacking in the ability to compete at high levels.

The head is short and refined, with a dish-shaped profile and a tapered muzzle with large nostrils. The eyes are large, wide-spaced and low-set, and the ears small, shapely and set well apart. The jaw is rounded and forms a curved arch where head and neck meet; this is known as the *mitbah*.

The back is slightly concave with sloping shoulders and well-defined withers. The croup is level and the girth deep. The tail is set high. The legs are strong, hard and clean with flat knees, short cannons, and well-defined tendons; the hooves are hard and tough. The Arab also has a distinctive skeletal feature in that it has fewer vertebrae, i.e. 5 lumbar, 17 rib, and 16 tail, compared with 6-18-18 in other breeds, giving it a short-coupled appearance. The horse's action is as if it were floating on air. Due to its desert origins, it has a fine coat and skin which is designed to release heat. Consequently, it requires special care in

winter, although Arabs are still tougher than Thoroughbreds.

Arabs are famous for their intelligence and responsiveness. They are also affectionate and respectful of other animals and human beings, being especially good with children. The reverse side of their character is fiery and courageous; they can also be stubborn if asked to do something against their will.

All solid colours are possible, but chestnut and grey are most common. Arabs stand between 14 and 15.2hh.

The Arab is an ancient breed whose hot blood has been used to improve many other breeds. It was of primary importance in the development of the Thoroughbred.

ARDENNAIS (France)

This ancient breed originated in the border country between France and Belgium, though it is regarded as French. A heavy draft horse, it is thought to be descended from the prehistoric Diluvial Horse of Solutré and was highly prized by the Romans, probably evolving into the great warhorse of the Middle Ages. In later centuries it continued to be used as a cavalry horse and was part of Napoleon's invasion of Russia in 1812, its extreme hardiness enabling it to cope with the harsh Russian winters.

The original Ardennais was fairly small, but its size and shape was increased The Ardennais is one of the heavier of the draft breeds. It can still be seen at work in French and Belgian fields.

by breeding it with the much larger Belgian Brabant to produce the horse we see today, this being one of enormous

strength and stamina. By the 19th century, further breeds had been added, such as Arab, Thoroughbred, French Boulonnais and Percheron, resulting in three distinctive types: the old original type of around 15hh; the much larger and heavier Trait du Nord; and the Auxois, which is very heavy, and is by far the most removed from the original. The Ardennais is still used as a heavy draft horse today.

One of the heaviest of the heavy draft types, the head of the Ardennais is unusually quite fine; the ears are small and wide apart, the eyes are prominent and friendly, and the nose is straight. The neck is quite short, broad and very strong, as is the back. The legs are short and thick-set.

The Ardennais has been bred to perform heavy work, which is evident in all aspects of its conformation. It is good-natured and obedient.

The most common coat colour is strawberry roan, with distinctive black points, though any other solid colour is acceptable apart from black. Height is between 15 and 16hh.

AUSTRALIAN PONY (Australia)

Many horses were imported during the colonization of Australia and they became an important part of Australian life. Ponies were also imported but were not paid any particular attention until the late 19th century, when a breed type began to emerge. By the 1920s this was starting to be recognized, and a stud book was started a little later on.

The Australian Pony is a combination of many breeds: Welsh, Arab, Thoroughbred, Shetland and Exmoor, to name but a few. These are now so intermingled that no single characteristic is uppermost, apart, perhaps, from the Welsh and Arab influences which can be seen in fine heads and neat legs. The result is an excellent all-rounder – good at jumping and agile enough for children's riding events; it is also perfect for trail-riding and endurance events.

The head is the pony's most striking feature and is evidence of its Arab ancestry. The ears are spaced well apart, being short and well-shaped; the forehead is broad and the eyes are large and kindly; the nose is slightly concave with slightly flared nostrils, leading down to a fine muzzle. The neck is well-developed with a silky, flowing mane; the withers are fairly pronounced and flow into a longish back with well-developed quarters; the legs are fine and tapered with strong tendons and short cannons and the hooves are hard and shapely.

The Australian Pony is fairly lightweight and its hotblood ancestry is immediately obvious. It is, however, extremely hardy and has great stamina. It is known for its sound constitution and is therefore easy to care for and ideal for children, being good-natured and obedient. Its most striking attribute is its free-flowing action.

The Australian has many of the characteristics of its Arab ancestors, including strength and stamina. It is an excellent all-rounder and is also popular for pony-trekking, where its sure-footedness is a great asset.

The ponies may be any colour, with white on the head and legs but not on the body. The most common colour is grey. Height is between 12 and 14hh.

AUSTRALIAN STOCK HORSE (Australia)

The Australian Stock Horse, otherwise known as the Waler, has a history that began in the 18th century, when horses were imported into Australia from South Africa and Chile. These tended to have excellent constitutions, being descended not only from Iberian, Arab, Barb, Criollo and Basuto stock, but also from Indonesian ponies. But the quality of the first horses was said to be not good enough, although later infusions of Arab and Thoroughbred brought great improvement to the stock.

The breed, also known as the New South Wales Horse, was once important as a cavalry horse, used by the British in India from about 1850, but soon became popular with stockmen where its soundness and endurance were assets in the huge expanses of the Australian outback; it was also used in harness.

By the 1940s the Waler, as it was now usually known, had become a quality horse, but after the Second World War the population was allowed to dwindle. It was bred with other horses which subsequently weakened the breed until it became rather inferior. Today, steps are being taken to improve the breed by using Quarter Horse, Arab and Thoroughbred, though, as yet, the Waler is not a consistent breed.

The ideal Waler has a fine head with a broad forehead, straight nose, and medium-length alert ears. The eyes are kind, inquisitive and intelligent. The neck is long and elegant, with a slight crest, and the shoulders are sloping. The chest is broad with a deep girth, while the body is of medium length with strong loins and well-developed quarters. The legs are strong with shapely hooves.

The Australian Stock Horse was predominantly used by stockmen, its hardiness and stamina being distinct assets on Australia's enormous sheep and cattle stations.

The Waler has excellent stamina and endurance. It is obedient and willing to work and is kind and intelligent.

Most often bays, all solid colours are possible. Height is 15–16.2hh.

AUXOIS (France)

The Auxois is closely related to French Ardennais stallions that were bred with Bourguignon mares, but infusions of Percheron and Boulonnais were added in the 19th century to further enhance the breed and to distinguish it from the Ardennais. The horse is still used in farming as well as in forestry, where its immense strength is harnessed in clearing trees. It has another role in the tourist industry, where it is used to draw gypsy caravans.

Similar to the Ardennais, the Auxois has a rather short, broad head with small alert ears and a kindly expression. The neck is well set on the shoulders and is short and muscular. The withers are well-defined with a broad chest, strong, sloping and muscular shoulders, and a short back and strong loins; the quarters are wide and well-developed with a low tail-carriage. The legs are short with large joints and a small amount of feathering. Despite its bulky appearance, the Auxois has a light and supple gait.

Strong and sturdy with plenty of stamina, the Auxois is a willing worker with an equable temperament.

The Auxois is a good all-round draft horse, used particularly in forestry work. Despite its bulk it is surprisingly agile.

Coat colour may be chestnut, bay, or red roan. The horse stands around 15–16hh.

BARB (North Africa)

The Barb has had an enormous influence on many breeds. It is of ancient origin, taking its name from the Barbary Coast of North Africa, which is now Morocco, Algeria, Tunisia and Libya, and where the Carthaginians bred cavalry horses 2,000 years ago. The breed was probably influenced at an early stage by Arab blood brought to North Africa by Muslims and also hotblooded Oriental types. A great many were imported to

Europe, particularly England, where there are many references to 'Barbary' horses, the most famous being Richard II's 'Roan Barbary'. Here they were also bred for the cavalry and were prized for their speed and stamina.

Nowadays, pure-bred Barbs are a rarity as the cross-breeding of Arabs and Barbs to produce good general riding horses is practised throughout North Africa. The Barb is not a handsome horse and is inclined to be bad-tempered, but it has had a tremendous influence on other breeds, particularly in Europe and the Americas. The Andalusian of Spain, the Connemara of Ireland, the

Sadly, few pure-bred Barbs remain, many of them having been crossed with Arabs to produce general riding horses.

Thoroughbred, and even the Criollo of South America, are all believed to contain Barb blood.

Today the Barb is used for general riding, racing, and display purposes. It remains very popular in its native land but receives little recognition elsewhere.

The Barb is fairly lightweight and bred for life in the desert. The head is long and narrow with a slightly dished face with medium well-shaped pointed ears; the eyes are kind and intelligent. The neck is of medium length with a pronounced crest. The withers are prominent and the shoulders flat. The legs are fine but strong, and the hooves are hard and well-shaped, a feature of all desert horses. The mane and tail are full with the tail set low on flat quarters.

The Barb is quite stand-offish and inclined to be bad-tempered. However, it has a reputation for extreme toughness, speed and stamina – qualities which have made it popular for improving other breeds.

Barbs are most commonly black, bay and dark brown, although Barbs with Arab blood can have other colours such as grey. Height is 14.2–15.2hh.

BASHKIR (Russia)

The Bashkir was once bred by the Bashkiri people of the lower slopes of the Urals to pull their troikas, while the mares' milk was used to make a fermented alcoholic drink called kumiss.

The breed is very old and has evolved in an extraordinary fashion: it has the stocky body, large head and small nostrils common to horses raised in very cold climates; but the strangest feature is its winter coat which grows to about 6in (15cm) in length and falls in tight ringlets.

In the United States, where there are approximately 1,500, they are known as Bashkir Curlies, some of which have recently been imported to the United Kingdom. Here they are mainly used in

showing and endurance riding, but in their native land they are used in harness and their long hair is spun into fabric; moreover, they are used for meat and their milk is still drunk. Another strange factor is the Bashkir's blood, which differs in composition from that of other horses; they also have higher respiratory and heart rates.

The original Bashkir has a large head with small ears. The eyes have an intelligent expression, the nose is straight, and the nostrils are small. The U.S. version has been bred to have a smaller head, which appears to balance more neatly on the body. The horse has a well-developed neck, longish body, and short stocky legs typical of horses from cold climates, where they develop a layer of fat to keep themselves extra warm in winter. In summer the coat is like that of any other horse, apart from the fact that the mane and tail remain curly.

These hardy animals are good-natured, affectionate and willing workers.

The most common colours are chestnut, palomino and bay. They stand at approximately 14hh.

The Bashkir is a very old breed, well-adapted to cold conditions. It grows a long, thick, curly coat to help it through harsh winters.

BASUTO (Lesotho)

The Basuto, or Basotho, from Lesotho, previously Basutoland, which is an enclave of South Africa, had its beginnings in the early 19th century and is derived from Arabs and Barbs which were brought to South Africa by Dutch settlers. Over the years they were allowed to became rather thin and scraggy in appearance and due to bad breeding their conformation deteriorated.

The breed virtually disappeared in the early 20th century when animals were exported and crossed with Thoroughbreds and Arabs to give them more substance. The Basuto was eventually saved by a society established in the later 20th century to improve and revive the breed. As well as the usual paces, the Basuto has two extra gaits, known as the triple and the pace.

The Basuto's head is rather large, with an underdeveloped, shortish neck. The body and legs are strong and wiry and the hooves are hard.

This horse is tough and can survive adverse conditions on very little food and water. It is only used for riding as all draft work in done by cattle. They come in all solid colours, as well as grey, and stand up to 14.1.

The Basuto possesses Arab and Barb bloodlines introduced by Dutch settlers in the 19th century.

BAVARIAN WARMBLOOD
(Germany)

The original Bavarian Warmblood was the Rottaler, a heavy horse bred from Norman and Oldenburg stallions. It was used for pulling carriages and for field work during the Second World War, when it was in great demand.

Today, the Bavarian Warmblood is something of an innovation, having received Rottaler mixed with Hanoverian, Westphalian, Trakehner and Bavarians have received Rottaler, Hanoverian, Westphalian, Trakehner and Thoroughbred bloodlines to create the perfect, versatile sports horse.

Thoroughbred bloodlines to produce a much lighter, more elegant warmblood sports horse capable of all disciplines. It was recognized as a breed in 1963.

This large elegant horse is similar in stature to the Hanoverian, though of a slightly lighter weight. It has a neat head, thick well-set neck, a heavy chest with a long sloping shoulder, and high withers. The back is fairly long and well-muscled, and the legs are strong with large hocks.

The Bavarian is a good-natured and willing worker. It has been bred to excel in all disciplines, which includes dressage, showjumping and eventing. The coat is usually chestnut in various shades. Height is approximately 16.2hh.

BELGIAN WARMBLOOD
(Belgium)

This is a relatively new breed, having been developed in the last century. It is the product of the selective breeding of Belgium's finest cavalry horses, as well as heavier breeds used in agriculture. It has been improved with Thoroughbreds and Anglo-Arabs as well as with other already established European warmbloods, such as the Hanoverian, Holstein, Selle Français and Dutch Warmblood. The result is a quality riding and competition horse which excels in international competition, particularly showjumping, eventing and dressage.

The Belgian Warmblood is near perfect in conformation and has many of the Thoroughbred characteristics. The head is of medium size with a straight nose and kind, alert eyes. The neck forms a graceful arch and is long and well-developed. The chest is substantial with a deep girth and sloping shoulder. The back is of medium length with muscular loins and powerful quarters. The legs are strong with large joints, and the hooves are well-shaped.

Belgian Warmbloods are much admired for their fluid paces, supple action and jumping ability. They are spirited and courageous as well as kind and willing. The coat comes in all solid colours. Height never deviates from between 16.1 and 16.2hh.

The Belgian Warmblood was created to be a sports horse, and can regularly be seen in top competitions, particularly dressage and showjumping. Those that don't quite make the grade, however, make fine riding horses.

BLACK FOREST (Germany)

The Black Forest is based on the ancient Noriker breed, a horse that was selected because of its capabilities in mountain regions, and was mated with other local breeds to produce the Black Forest. In 1896 an association and stud book were established to protect the breed, when it was stipulated that only Belgian Heavy Draft (Brabant) stallions could be bred with Black Forest mares, thus improving and enlarging the breed to make it a strong draft horse. Many farmers who did not approve of introducing Belgian Heavy Draft horses carried on using local native stallions, however, and even forged their foals' identity papers. By the early 1900s, the authorities finally recognized the Schwartzwald farmers' needs and they were allowed to carry on as they had before.

Today the breed has been standardized with around 700 mares and 45 stallions at the Marbach/Weil stud, state-owned by Baden-Württemburg, and which always has about 16 stallion standing at stud. The breed is still used not only in farming and forestry work, but also as a carriage horse and, because of its nimble and lively gait, often for riding.

In appearance, the Black Forest lies somewhere between a Haflinger and a Noriker. The head is medium-sized and fairly plain, with a straight or slightly

Roman nose and soft eyes. The neck is short, well-developed and strong, with a straight shoulder. The body is sturdy with sloping quarters and a low-set tail. The legs are short with plenty of bone and hard hooves that have a little feathering.

Black Forests are lively, agile and willing horses, most commonly seen as chestnuts with pale manes and tails – also as dark-silver dapples, which are the most popular. In height, they stand at around 15–16hh.

The Black Forest has much in common with the Noriker. Besides being a riding horse, it is not uncommon to see it working on farms and engaged in forestry work.

BOERPERD (South Africa)

The Boerperd, or Boer Horse, has a history that runs side by side with the white settlers of South Africa and the arrival of the Dutch in Cape Town in 1652. The first horses seen in the region were of Oriental blood and were imported from Java, which in turn were sold by the Dutch East India Company to the Free Burghers in 1665. Over the years, however, significant inbreeding had taken place, so measures were taken to improve the breed by introducing Arab blood to the stock.

This practice continued for 150 years until a definite type emerged, known as the Cape Horse. Meanwhile, some Iberian breeds arrived in the Cape in 1793, which may or may not have had an effect on the native horses. Cape Horses remained very popular into the late 18th and early 19th centuries and were prized for their endurance, stamina, speed and intelligence, which made them useful military horses.

Over the years, various other influences had an effect on the breed, such as Flemish horses, and Hackneys, Norfolk Trotters and Cleveland Bays further enhanced the breed. The horse continued to survive, despite disease and the Boer Wars in which it proved its worth, and

The Boerperd took its name from the Boer Wars in which it was widely used.

which finally gave the Boerperd its present name.

The Boerperd owes much of its appearance to its Arab and Oriental forebears. The head is small and wedge-shaped with a slightly dished or straight nose and a small, neat muzzle with flared nostrils. The eyes are bright and intelligent and the ears are medium-sized and alert. The body is short and compact with neatly sloping shoulders, a deep girth, and well-proportioned muscular legs with plenty of bone. The hooves are tough and shapely.

Boerperds are spirited, courageous and intelligent, with plenty of stamina and agility. Coats come in most solid colours and grey. Height is 14.2–15.2hh.

BOULONNAIS (France)

The ancient Boulonnais may have been bred from Numidian horses imported by Julius Caesar's army in around 54 BC, which were in evidence along the coast of the Pas-de-Calais prior to the invasion of the British Isles. Then came the Crusades and the Spanish occupation of Flanders, when other breeds with Oriental bloodlines, such as Arabs, Barbs and Andalusians, were introduced to the region and bred with the Roman-type horses to produce the original Boulonnais; infusions of Mecklenburg blood would later further shape the breed.

The Boulonnais is known as the 'thoroughbred' of draft horses because of its elegance, agility and turn of speed. It is well known for its spectacular gait, which made it popular as a carriage

horse; it was also a willing worker in the fields and was even used as a riding horse. It was most famous for a race known as *La route du poisson* (The Fish Route) which occurred every two years. It commemorated a time during the 17th century when it was used for the rapid transport of freshly caught fish from the English Channel to Paris in less than 24 hours.

The popularity of the breed has made it valuable in improving other heavy breeds, as well as providing the foundation blood for many competition horses.

There are two types of Boulonnais: the smaller 'fish-cart' horse which was used for the fish transportation and is now very rare and no larger than 15.3hh. Seen today, however, is the large type, with its large elegant head with wide forehead and slightly Roman nose, inquisitive eyes, wide nostrils, and small pricked ears. The neck is thick and muscular with a well-defined crest and a thick mane. The chest is wide with a deep, rounded rib cage. The withers sit deeply into the muscles of the shoulders and back. The back is straight and the legs are solid and strong; unlike many heavy breeds the legs have little hair.

It may be large but the Boulonnais has a surprising turn of speed.

Boulonnais are energetic, lively and enjoy work. They are usually grey, but the occasional chestnut may occur. There is currently a breeding programme to produce other colours – particularly black. Their height is around 16.3hh.

BRABANT (Belgium)

The Brabant, or Belgian Heavy Draft
Horse, comes from the area of Belgium
that has Brussels as its capital. It is of
ancient origin, only slightly more recent
than the Ardennais to which it owes part
of its lineage: the other part of its
inheritance is thought to have stemmed
from the Flanders Horse of the 11th to
16th centuries, which in turn is believed to
be descended from the ancient horses of
the Quaternary period. For centuries
Belgian breeders produced their stock by
selective breeding, which also included
inbreeding.

The Brabant's very existence is a
direct result of the geology of the area, in
that the rich, heavy soil required a horse
with great pulling power and big strong
joints to enable it to lift its huge feet out
of the thick clods of mud. As a result,
three distinct bloodlines emerged 100
years ago, which intermingled to create
the modern Brabant: the Gros de la
Dendre, which is muscular and strong
with huge legs; the Gris de Nivelles,
with good conformation and a certain
elegance; and the Colosse de la Mehaigne,
which is large and has a lively
temperament.

Over the centuries, the Brabant has
had enormous influence on today's
modern breeds, much in the same way as
the Arab bloodline has been added to

improve existing stock. In the Middle
Ages the horse was imported all over
Europe and its bloodlines are present in
the German warmbloods. The Russians
introduced native breeds to it to produce
working horses and its influence is also
present in the Shire, Irish Draft and
Clydesdale, to name but a few. Today,
Brabants are still part of the foundation
stock for the breeding of warmbloods.
They now appear throughout the world
where they are still used in agricultural

work, in logging and as dray horses. They can also be seen in the show ring.

The head is fairly square with a straight profile, small pricked ears, and deeply-set eyes with a kindly expression. The neck is short and very strong and is set high with a large crest. The shoulders are sloping and the chest is wide and deep. The body is short with a well-muscled back and strong quarters. The legs are fairly long and muscular and the hooves are large, rounded and tough; there is not much feathering present.

The Brabant is an extremely docile animal, to the point that it could almost be described as sluggish. However, it has an equable nature, is obedient, and possesses pulling power equal only to the Shire's, for which it is highly prized. It is a hard worker with plenty of stamina and a

The Brabant is an ancient draft horse, bred for working the heavy soil of its native land. It is still used in farm and forestry work today.

strong constitution, and requires relatively little food for its size.

Most commonly light chestnut with a flaxen mane, red roan, bay, dun and grey are also acceptable coat colours. Height is around 16.1–17hh.

BRANDENBURG (Germany)

A stud at Neustadt was founded in the late 18th century and it was here that the Brandenburg was developed. The breeding programme resulted in a warmblooded horse that was heavy enough for use on farms but sufficiently elegant to pull carriages.

By the end of the Second World War the breed was reassessed and using Hanoverian and Trakehner stallions the Brandenburg was remodelled into the lighter warmblood sports horse much in demand today. The Brandenburg excels at dressage, showjumping, eventing and driving.

The attractive head is fine and medium-sized, set neatly onto a medium-length, well-formed neck. The back is straight and strong with rather a long croup. The legs are strong, straight and of medium length.

The Brandenburg is kind and even-tempered; it is also obedient and a willing worker. It is predominantly bay in colour and stands at 16.2hh.

The Brandenburg was originally bred to work as a carriage horse and on farms. Today, however, it is used exclusively as a riding and sports horse.

BRETON (France)

The Breton originated in a department of north-west France called Bretagne (Brittany). The breed standard was formed quite recently, but the history of the breed's development goes back 4,000 years, when the Aryans introduced Asian stock to Europe. In Brittany, the demanding climate and poor-quality terrain caused local horses to adapt to their environment, resulting in horses that possessed great strength and durability. The Breton is therefore the result of evolution over hundreds of years, and long periods of selection carried out by breeders using old varieties of native horses.

Brittany has a long history of breeding distinguished horses which stretches back to the Middle Ages; in fact, the Breton horse was much prized by military leaders around the time of the Crusades, even though the breed was small at only 14hh. The Crusaders' Oriental horses, which they brought back with them from the East, were then bred with the Brittany horses to produce two separate strains: the Sommier, a slow packhorse, and the Roussin, used for riding and as a warhorse. The two types remained popular for centuries, and by the 18th century had been crossed with Ardennais, Boulonnais and Percheron to produce a much larger, stronger animal, which was known as the Grand Breton.

By the 19th century infusions of Norfolk Trotter, along with Hackney, had been introduced to produce a lighter but still substantial animal useful for light draft and military work; when used as a carriage horse it was known as the Postier-Breton. As well as the Grand Breton and the Postier Breton there is another type, the Corlay Breton, developed from crossings with Arabs and Thoroughbreds and which is probably the nearest to the original horse of Brittany, being no bigger than 15hh.

The head is square with a heavy jaw. The ears are small and expressive and the eyes bright and kind. The nose is straight, though slightly dished in the Corlay Breton, and the nostrils are large. The neck is short with a well-developed crest, the short-coupled body being wide and muscular, as is the croup. The shoulders are long and the legs are short and muscular with strong cannon bones.

All three Breton types have equable natures and are willing workers. They are extremely hardy and have plenty of stamina, making them easy to maintain.

They are mostly chestnuts, but roans, bays and greys are also acceptable. Sizes range from 14.3hh (Corlay) to 16hh (Grand Breton).

The Breton is probably France's most popular heavy horse, and although the breed standard is relatively new, its history dates back many thousands of years.

BRITISH WARMBLOOD (U.K.)

The warmblood horse has been of particular importance to British competition for a very long time and is the result of Thoroughbreds crossed with Irish Drafts. These make excellent eventers and showjumpers and have been proving their worth since the middle of the 20th century, when equestrian sports began to take off in earnest.

One aspect of equestrianism in which the United Kingdom did not excel was dressage. The sport had long been popular in Europe, where European warmbloods were especially bred for the purpose. Over the last 30 years or so, however, the discipline had been gaining popularity in the United Kingdom as British riders have become more interested in dressage as a sport. It was necessary for them to continue to use European warmbloods, but it was eventually felt that Britain should have a warmblood of her own, which led to the formation of the British Warmblood Society in 1977.

British competitors take their sports extremely seriously, which is reflected in the care they exercise over the equine athletes that compete in them. In Britain, besides the British Warmblood Society, there are two other such organizations – the British Hanoverian Horse Society, and the Trakehner Breeders' Fraternity.

The term 'warmblood' loosely describes a wide range of breeds from all over Europe, each with their own specific set of criteria. It is generally understood that true warmbloods are of European stock and not the Thoroughbred-Irish cross which is technically a warmblood but not recognized as such.

The British Warmblood is based on various European bloodlines, but so far the breed is not consistent, even though registration of these animals is strictly controlled with only the very best being recognized. The British Warmblood continues to enjoy great success in dressage and jumping.

Because the British Warmblood breeding programme is still in its infancy there is no consistent type. But generally speaking their appearance fits the standards of most European warmbloods.

These horses are kind and intelligent and like most warmbloods are obedient and enjoyable to ride.

All solid colours, with white on the face and legs, are acceptable. Height is 15–16.3hh.

The British Warmblood was created to compete with the other warmblood sports horses of Europe.

BRUMBY (Australia)

Brumbies are free-roaming feral horses, and although they are found in many areas in Australia, the majority of them live in the Northern Territory today, with the second largest population in Queensland. There are more horses living in the wild in Australia than in any other country of the world, and they even outnumber America's famous Mustang.

A herd of Brumbies is known as a 'mob' or a 'band'.

Australia had no native horses of her own until they were introduced during the country's gradual colonization, and in

particular by settlers who arrived during the 19th-century gold rush. Not only was there an influx of people, therefore, but also of animals, and this included the horses which came with them. During the First World War, many of the horses escaped or were turned loose to run wild: these were the forefathers of the modern-day Brumby, a name said to be derived from the aboriginal word for wild (*baroomby*).

Because of the variety of animals which reverted to a wild state, there is no specific breed type; consequently Brumbies come in all shapes, sizes and colours.

Brumbies are prolific breeders and for this reason have come to be regarded as pests. This has led to such extensive culling that they are now quite rare.

Today, some live in National Parks. and others are occasionally rounded up and domesticated for use as working stock on farms or stations – also as trail horses, show horses, Pony Club mounts and pleasure horses.

The Brumby comes in all varieties, including dun, roan and coloured. Height is around 15hh.

Australia had no native breeds of her own; horses were introduced by settlers, who turned them loose and left them to run wild.

BUDENNY (Russia)

The Budenny, or Budyonny, is a relatively young breed, having been created by the Russians to fit the basic criteria of a Perfect Russian Horse, a standard which is centuries old. A Russian horse should be an excellent all-rounder, equally at home being ridden as pulling a carriage. Development of the breed began in 1921 when the devastation of the First World War and the Russian Revolution made it clear that a good cavalry horse was

The Buddenny was originally used as a cavalry horse, but is today a general riding and sports horse.

required. The horse was named after Marshal Budenny (1883–1973), who was responsible for the breed's development.

As a cavalry horse it was obliged to satisfy a number of requirements: it needed enormous stamina, a good turn of speed, and the ability to jump; obedience and an equable nature were also needed, as well as great courage. The breeding programme took place at Rostov, where there was a military stud. The breed is based on Don and Chernomor mares crossed with Thoroughbred stallions; Chernomors are similar to Dons, though rather lighter. They also introduced Kazakh and Kirgiz bloodlines, though with less success. The breed was eventually recognized and was registered in 1949.

Today the Budenny is used as a performance horse and in all disciplines, including racing, endurance, and showjumping. It is also used in harness.

The Budenny bears a close resemblance to the Thoroughbred, being tall and powerful with good bone and muscle. The head is medium-sized and sits well on the neck. The nose is straight or slightly concave and the nostrils are wide. The ears are of medium size and the eyes are bold. The neck is long and set high and the withers are also high. The back is fairly short and is inclined to flatten towards the withers. The loins are

wide, medium-length and muscular. The croup is usually long. The shoulder is of medium length and sloping. The legs are clean and strong and the hooves well-shaped and hard.

Due to its military breeding, the Budenny has plenty of courage and spirit.

It is also obedient and has a good disposition.

Budennys are nearly always chestnut, with an iridescent sheen to the coat inherited from the Don. Bays and browns occasionally appear. They are usually around 16hh.

CAMARGUE (France)

The horses that inhabit the salt marshes and lagoons of the Rhône delta in southeast France are semi-wild and spend much of their time grazing the sparse vegetation. They are very ancient and are probably descended from the Diluvial Horse. They also bear a striking resemblance to the primitive horses painted in the caves at Lascaux in prehistoric times; it is also likely that Oriental and Barb blood runs in their veins because of their facial shape.

The breed was further enhanced in the 19th century by the introduction of Postier Breton, Arab, Anglo-Arab and Thoroughbred bloodlines, though these additions seem to have had little bearing on the horses' overall appearance.

There is an annual round-up in the Camargue when suitable horses are selected for riding purposes, while the weaker and substandard colts and stallions are culled: this may seem ruthless but there is no doubt that it has led to improvements in the breed.

Camargue horses are traditionally ridden by the *gardiens*, who use them for herding the famous black bulls of the region and for festivals in which their dazzling horsemanship is displayed. The horses are also used for trekking the region, now a popular tourist attraction.

The head is rather square, with a broad forehead, short, broad ears, and

HORSES

Camargues are usually grey in colour, although bays and browns occasionally appear. Foals are born dark but become grey as they mature. They stand at around 13.1–14.2hh in height.

OPPOSITE: It is thought that Camargues are descended from the Diluvial Horse.

LEFT: Camargue foals are born dark, but usually lighten to the distinctive grey (white) as they mature.

BELOW: Camargue horses are ridden by the *gardiens*, who use them to herd the black bulls of the region.

expressive eyes. The neck is short and well-developed, the shoulder is upright, and the back is short with a low-set tail. The legs are strong and the hooves well-shaped and tough. The mane and tail are long and abundant.

Camargues make obedient and willing riding horses; they are extremely agile and have the ability to make sharp turns at a full gallop. They are also sure-footed and have plenty of stamina, making them suitable as trekking ponies for the many visitors to the region. However, they have never quite lost their independent spirit and continue to retain something of their wild inheritance.

CARTHUSIAN (Spain)

The Carthusian shares much of its history with the Andalusian. In the mid-15th century the Carthusian monks of Jerez de la Frontera were bequeathed 10,000 acres (4,000 hectares) of grazing land, which they used for the selective breeding of the highly revered Iberian horses, being determined to preserve the pure Iberian blood. When the monarch insisted on Neapolitan being added to the stock they flatly refused and continued to breed their fine Spanish horses. In 1808–14 Napoleon invaded the peninsula and stole many of the best of the stock. The monks, in an attempt to preserve the breed, rescued the remaining horses and from these few the modern, fairly heavy Andalusian emerged, also the Carthusian, which was Iberian mixed with Arab and Barb to produce a lighter breed.

The Carthusian is slightly smaller than the Andalusian and not as heavy. The head is broad with a straight, noble profile and widely-spaced alert ears. The eyes are large and intelligent.

Intelligent and good-natured as well as being spirited and courageous, Carthusians are easy to handle, complaisant and obedient.

They are usually grey, but occasionally chestnuts and blacks appear. Height is up to 15hh.

The Carthusian is lesser known than the Andalusian, though no less important.

CASPIAN (Iran)

The Caspian is claimed to be the oldest breed of all and its history would seem to bear this out. Although domesticated, its bloodline is remarkably pure, with descent that appears to have been traced from a prehistoric Oriental horse. Fossils of a horse of this type were found in Iran which are almost exact matches of the bone structure of today's Caspian. A likeness of the horse can also be seen on a seal belonging to Darius the Great, who ruled Persia (Iran) in around 500 BC. The Caspian is probably the prototype of the Arab horse, Caspian blood being consequently in many of today's breeds.

This small horse is thought to have become extinct in around the 10th century, so it was all the more amazing to discover a herd of 40 of them roaming in the remote Elburz Mountains in 1965. They were shipped to England, which was the start of studs being formed all over the world, and which is where a breed society was established to preserve this rare and ancient breed. Nowadays, the Caspian's small stature makes it an ideal horse for children and its even temperament means that it is equally suitable for beginners.

Typical of the Oriental type, the head is small and fine with small, alert ears and

a straight nose with large nostrils. The eyes are large and intelligent. The strong, elegant neck is set quite high; the shoulders are sloping and the body is of medium proportions though quite narrow.

The Caspian, though pony-like in stature, has the heart of a horse. It also has all the qualities needed to make it an excellent riding horse, being affectionate, intelligent and obedient. It is far from dull and has plenty of spirit. It would also makes a good driving pony. Caspians are usually bay, chestnut or grey and are between 10–12hh in height.

The Caspian is possibly the oldest breed in the world and was thought to have become extinct in the 10th century. Amazingly, a small herd of them was discovered in the 1960s, wandering free in an isolated mountain valley in Iran.

CAYUSE (U.S.A.)

The Cayuse is very different from other American breeds which more often than not are descended from Spanish and Arab horses brought over by the conquistadors in the 16th century. The Cayuse's ancestry is practically unknown, but it is generally thought to be descended from French horses, probably Percherons, which were imported to Canada in the 1600s; Percherons were popular with the Canadians, who used them to improve their own workhorses.

It was the French Canadians who introduced their horses to America, where there are records that they bartered them with Pawnee Indians in St. Louis. Consequently, it was the Native Americans who bred these heavy horses with Spanish and Oriental blood to produce a horse capable of speed, strength and endurance.

In the 1800s the Cayuse was established as a separate breed and it was again the Native Americans, who were superb horsemen, who continued to refine the breed through selective breeding. Strangely, it is the Percheron throwback which produces the spots and markings which often appear on the Cayuse; in turn, the Cayuse has influenced both the Paint and Appaloosa horses.

HORSES

Today the Cayuse is rare and exists only in California, where great efforts are being made to preserve the breed.

The Cayuse has many of the attributes of its Spanish inheritance, having a fine head with a straight nose, small ears, and kind eyes. The neck is medium-length and well-developed, with rather high withers and a good sloping shoulder. The body is strong and sturdy with short but strong legs, probably a legacy of its Percheron forebears. The sloping pasterns make it capable of performing a broken walk, which is most comfortable for riders over long distances.

Small, stocky and very strong, but with all the nobility and bearing of its Spanish forebears.

The Cayuse was the favourite horse of Native Americans, who improved the breed through selective breeding. Today, however, it is very rare, and exists only in California.

The Cayuse comes in all solid colours, and there are also coloureds and spotteds. Height is around 14hh.

CLEVELAND BAY (U.K.)

The excellent Cleveland Bay is Britain's oldest breed and dates back to medieval times. Gradually, however, it became more rare, and numbers dipped to a critical level in the last century. Thankfully, it is once more gaining in popularity and numbers have begun to increase.

The breed is related to the Chapman Horse which lived in north-east Yorkshire in the Middle Ages and which received Iberian and Barb bloodlines. Clevelands were then used mainly as packhorses and for agricultural work, being greatly admired for their strength and ability to carry heavy loads for long distances. The name comes from the area (Cleveland) where they were bred and the fact that their colour is bay.

Later the breed was crossed with Thoroughbred to produce the lighter, elegant carriage horse which is a feature of the Cleveland Bay today. Sadly the previous type is now extinct.

In a previous age the Cleveland Bay was very popular, but the development of motorized transport saw its demise and by the 1970s the breed had been reduced to an all-time low. In some respects, however, it is still very much in evidence; Cleveland Bays have been kept at the royal mews since King George V introduced them there, and the

HORSES

Hampton Court Stud still actively breeds the horses to be used in state and ceremonial occasions.

Today Cleveland Bays and part-breds can be seen in showjumping, dressage, eventing, driving and hunting, where they are admired for their sure-footedness and great stamina.

Clevelands have large, noble heads on long muscular necks, which are attached to sloping shoulders and long, deep bodies. The strong, shortish legs have plenty of bone and no feathers.

Calm and intelligent and seemingly possessing the ability to think for themselves, Clevelands are honest, strong

Once rare, the Cleveland Bay is beginning to benefit from a renewal of interest in the breed.

and confident horses, with enormous powers of endurance.

Exclusively bay, with rich black manes and tails and black-stockinged legs with no white, they stand between 16 and 17hh.

CLYDESDALE (U.K.)

The establishment of the Clydesdale began in the late-17th century when Lanarkshire farmers and various dukes of Hamilton supposedly imported Flemish stallions, ancestors of the Brabant, to Scotland. The farmers were skilful breeders and mated them with native heavy draft mares already in existence; over the next 100 years or so, English Shire, Friesian and Cleveland Bay blood was also added. The result was known as the Clydesdale and it was highly prized as a draft horse. The Clydesdale Horse Society was established in 1877, almost a century and a half after the breed first began to evolve.

The breed soon became popular as a general farm horse and also for haulage over long and short distances; Clydesdales could be found in most major cities of Scotland, the North of England and Northern Ireland, as well as in agricultural areas. In fact, the horse became popular the world over, when considerable numbers were imported to North America, Canada and Australia.

The Clydesdale differs from most heavy draft horses, which tend to be squat and plain-looking; in fact, with its short-coupled body, long legs, and high head-carriage it looks positively refined.

As with all heavy horses the Clydesdale breed began to decline with the development of motorized transport and reached an even lower ebb in the 1960s and 70s. However, a few families kept the breed going and today numbers have increased though the horse is still classified as 'at risk' by the Rare Breeds Society. Today they are highly valued in the show ring as well as in harness and as dray horses, where they take part in displays and are even used to pull wedding carriages.

The head is proudly held with medium, well-shaped ears which are pricked and alert; the eyes are kind and intelligent. The nose is slightly Roman and the nostrils large. The neck is long and well-set, with a high crest leading to high withers. The back is slightly concave and short and the quarters are well-developed and powerful. The legs are straight and long with plenty of feathering. The feet are large and require careful shoeing to prevent contracted heels from developing.

These charming horses are energetic with an alert, cheerful air. They are even-tempered and enjoy the company of other horses and human beings. They are extremely strong with a lively action and a slight tendency to dish.

Clydesdales can be bay, brown and black and usually have white patches all the way up the legs and under the belly, which can turn roan in places. They are usually 16.2hh, but some males may reach 17hh or more.

It was common, a couple of hundred years ago, for Clydesdales to be seen working on farms or hauling loads over great distances. Sadly their numbers dwindled, placing them in danger of extinction. Fortunately, they are now on the increase and can be seen in the show ring or being used for such happy occasions as pulling wedding carriages.

COMTOIS (France)

The Comtois is an ancient coldblooded breed which is thought to have been brought to France by the Burgundians, a Germanic people who invaded Gaul in the 5th century and established their kingdom in east-central France, centred on Dijon.

The Comtois originated in the Franche-Comté and Jura mountains on the borders of France and Switzerland. By the 16th century the breed was used to improve Burgundian horses, which gained a good reputation as warhorses in the cavalry of Louis XIV and were also used by Napoleon in his invasion of Russia. It

The Comtois has plenty of stamina, its sure-footed confidence making it an asset in mountain regions.

was bred with other draft breeds in the 19th century, such as Boulonnais and Percherons, to produce a heavier horse; by the early 20th century it was further improved using Ardennais stallions.

Nowadays the Comtois is also bred in the Massif Central, the Pyrenees, and the Alps, where its stamina and sure-footedness makes it perfectly suited to the mountainous terrain, and where it is used for hauling logs and for work in vineyards. It is the second most popular draft breed in France after the Breton.

The Comtois is lightly built for a draft horse. The head is large, the eyes alert and intelligent, and the ears small and neat. The neck is short and well-developed and the body is stocky and powerful with a deep girth. The back is long and straight with muscular hindquarters. The legs are short and strong with small amounts of feathering. Mane and tail are full.

The Comtois is very hardy and lives to a ripe old age. It is good-natured, obedient and hard-working.

They usually appear in various shades of chestnut, with flaxen manes and tails – also as browns or bays. Height is between 14.1 and 15.1hh.

CONNEMARA (Ireland)

The Connemara is Ireland's only native breed, although it is not indigenous to the country. It is thought that it was brought to Ireland 2,500 years ago when the Celts settled in Ireland and brought their ponies with them. The Celts were traders and travelled to and from Mediterranean ports, which makes it likely that their ponies were of Oriental descent, probably Barb. In medieval times these were bred with the Irish Hobeye, which was a much coveted riding horse, famous for its speed, agility and endurance.

Legend has it that further blood was added to the breed when the Spanish Armada sunk off the coast of Ireland and Iberian horses swam ashore and mated with native breeds. Later the breed was further improved with infusions of Hackney, Welsh Cob, Irish Draft, Clydesdale and Thoroughbred.

The Connemara derives its name from the region of that name which, a few hundred years ago, included Connaught and Galway, and where the terrain is rocky and mountainous with very little vegetation. The weather can be atrocious, with piercing winds and

The Connemara makes an excellent child's competition pony, particularly as it is a naturally good jumper.

driving rain coming in off the Atlantic. Consequently, the Connemara has evolved into an extremely hardy specimen, which is sure-footed and agile and has extraordinary jumping abilities.

Historically, it was used as a draft horse, transporting peat and seaweed as well as taking potatoes and corn to market. Nowadays it is used for hunting, eventing, showjumping and driving; it is often crossed with the Thoroughbred to produce an excellent jumping horse.

The Connemara is a riding pony of excellent quality. The head is fine and set quite high, with small pricked ears, clever eyes, and a straight nose with fairly large nostrils. The neck is of medium length and well-muscled and the shoulders are sloping, with a deep girth, a straight back, and well-developed quarters. The legs are short but elegant, being strong with very hard hooves.

Connemaras are often bred with Thoroughbreds to produce jumping horses.

The Connemara is intelligent with a calm and kindly disposition. It is an excellent all-rounder and being hardy is easy to maintain.

They are most commonly grey, but bay, black, dun and brown may also appear. They stand at around 13–14.2hh.

CRIOLLO (Argentina)

The Spanish conquistadors were responsible for the existence of the horse in the Americas and what better stock to introduce than the Arab, Barb and excellent Iberian. It is these three bloodlines which make up the Criollo, the native horse of Argentina. For many hundreds of years it roamed the plains (pampas) of Argentina, where extreme conditions of heat and cold resulted in the natural selection of horses that are among the toughest in the world.

The Criollo became the horse of the gaucho, or South American cowboy, who quickly recognized its excellent qualities of hardiness, stamina, speed and resilience (they were also used as packhorses).

Criollos are now the subject of a selective breeding programme designed to preserve the horse's special features. In Argentina this entails an annual breeders' test in which the horses travel for 750 miles (1200km) for 15 days carrying 242lb (110kg), their only food and drink being what they can forage for themselves en route.

Today, herds of these horses live in semi-wild conditions on the enormous ranches of South America, where they are caught and broken in as required. They are still used as stock and riding horses, and when crossed with Thoroughbreds make excellent polo ponies.

The horse's toughness is apparent from its stocky exterior. The head is broad with wide-apart eyes and a slightly dished nose; it has fairly large ears. The neck is well-developed with a wide back and chest and strong quarters. The back is short with sloping shoulders and the short, sturdy legs have plenty of bone.

The Criollo is tough, can survive on next to nothing, and is an obedient worker. It is able to withstand some of the harshest conditions in the world.

These young Criollo horses are allowed to run wild in the foothills of Mount Lanin in Patagonia until they are old enough for breaking in.

The horses are most commonly dun-coloured, with black manes and tails, eel stripes down the centres of their backs, and with zebra markings on the legs. Other possible colours are chestnut, bay, black, roan, grey, piebald, skewbald and palomino. They are 14–15hh in height.

DALES (U.K.)

The Dales pony is the only British native breed which has never been completely wild. Its earliest descendant is the Celtic Pony, though it was elements of the sure-footed Scottish Galloway, used as a pack pony and which worked in the lead mines situated high on the moors, which truly gave birth to the breed. Further improvements came with infusions of Friesian, Welsh Cob and Clydesdale.

The Dales pony is a native of the upper dales of the eastern slopes of the Pennine range, from the High Peak in Derbyshire to the Cheviot Hills near to the Scottish Border, and is often confused with the similar Fell pony from the western side of the Pennines; before the breeds were split they were collectively known as Pennine ponies.

The Dales pony proved popular and comfortable to ride and was strong enough for draft work. It had excellent stamina and was able to thrive on the bleak uplands of the dales. They were the versatile workhorses of the hill farmers, perfect for small farms and capable of pulling cartloads of a ton or more. They were also used as shepherds' ponies and could cover great distances with burdens of 170lb (77kg) or more, often with a rider as well, and in deep snow. When not working around the farm they were also used for days out hunting, and where their jumping skills were much in evidence.

Today, Dales ponies feature in showing classes – also in trekking and in harnessed driving competitions.

They have neat heads, which are broad between the eyes, which are bright

The Dales is strong and hardy, making it an excellent riding and driving pony for adults and children alike.

and alert. The ears are small and curve slightly inwards. The Dales's trademark is its long forlock, which hangs down the

centre of the face. The neck is fairly long and well-developed, with a long, thick mane. The body is short with a deep girth, sloping shoulders and well-developed hindquarters. The legs are sturdy with feathers around the fetlocks.

The Dales pony is extremely tough, its strong legs and feet and sturdy body allowing it to cope with heavy loads. Being hardy, it is undaunted by adverse weather conditions. It is also alert, with a quiet intelligence, and is a willing worker.

Dales ponies are usually black, with some bays, browns and greys and very occasionally roans. White should be confined to a star or snip on the face, with only a little on the fetlocks of the hindlegs. Height is up to 14.2hh.

DANISH WARMBLOOD

(Denmark)

The story of the Danish Warmblood begins in Holstein which, until the mid-19th century, was Danish territory and afforded the Danes easy access to German warmblood stock through the Cistercian monasteries of Holstein. For centuries the monks had been breeding the old-style heavy Holstein with highly-bred Iberian stallions to produce useful multi-purpose horses; these practices were therefore far from new.

The Royal Frederiksborg Stud, which was founded in 1562 near Copenhagen, was already breeding Andalusians and Neapolitans, and this stock was interbred with a small Danish breed and the larger Jutland Heavy Draft (both coldbloods), with infusions of Turkish and Dutch breeds and later additions of English Thoroughbred. This created the excellent all-rounder known as the Frederiksborg (page 122), for which the monks of Holstein had long been striving. The stud closed in 1862, but some of the stock survived in the hands of private breeders.

Excelling as a sports horse of superb quality and ability, the Danish Warmblood was established in the 20th century as a rival to other European breeds.

By the middle of the 20th century the Danes realized they needed to create a competition sports horse of superb quality to rival other European breeds. Subsequently, they decided to breed the Frederiksborg-Thoroughbred mares with Thoroughbred, Anglo-Norman, Trakehner, Wielkopolski and Malopolski stallions to create the truly superb Danish Warmblood. It is interesting to note that Hanoverian was not used, which is unusual, as it is present in most other European warmblood breeds.

These horses are the supreme masters of high-level competition, though the less talented still make wonderful all-purpose riding horses. They particularly excel at dressage and showjumping.

The conformation of the Danish Warmblood is near-perfect: it has a noble head with large, intelligent eyes and fairly long, tapered ears. All elements of the body are in perfect proportion, from the long, well-developed neck to the straight well-boned legs and shapely feet.

Admired for its fluid paces and supple action, which make it so popular as a dressage horse, the Danish Warmblood is spirited and courageous but at the same time kind and willing.

They are most commonly bays but all solid colours are acceptable. A little white is permitted on the head and legs. Height is 16.1–16.2hh.

DANUBIAN (Bulgaria)

The Danubian is a relatively new breed which was established in the early 20th century. The aim of the Bulgarian breeders was to produce a sensible light draft and riding horse by mating the larger, heavier types of Nonius stallions with the higher-quality Gidrán mares to produce offspring that were strong and sturdy with excellent stamina and endurance. But the Nonius genes are rather dominant, and despite various other breedings with Arabs and Thoroughbreds, the Danubian still displays the rather mundane attributes of the original stallions, even though the Nonius is renowned for its even temperament, strength and ability.

Today the Danubian is still used as a riding and light draft horse and is often crossed with Thoroughbreds to produce performance horses.

The head is rather plain but with good proportions. The ears are of medium length and the eyes smallish. The body is chunky and sturdy, being rather cobby, with a shortish well-developed neck, strong shoulders and a deep girth. The legs are well-muscled at the tops and have plenty of bone.

RIGHT: These are Dartmoor ponies living in their wild state, though they are closely monitored to ensure the survival of the breed.

The Danubian is a sensible, willing worker, with plenty of stamina and endurance. It is kind and easy to handle. It usually comes in dark chestnut or black. Height is around 15.2hh.

DARTMOOR (U.K.)

There is evidence that ponies inhabited Dartmoor as early as 2000 BC, a fact confirmed by remains excavated on Shaugh Moor. The earliest written reference to the Dartmoor is in the will of Awifold of Credition, who died in 1012. Stemming from Celtic Ponies which bred with other British natives, there were later additions of Roadster, Welsh Pony, Cob, Arab, and more recently Thoroughbred.

The Dartmoor pony comes from the county of Devon in the south-west of England, taking its name from the area of wild moorland where it still roams free. Standing over 1,000ft (305m) above sea level, with wind and rain driving off the sea, it can be an inhospitable place with rocky outcrops and sparse vegetation. Consequently, the pony is extremely hardy and sure-footed and has plenty of stamina.

Dartmoors fail to thrive, however, if left solely to their own devices and require hay in the winter, which farmers put out for them. This was confirmed during the Second World War when Dartmoor was completely out of bounds. As a result, the population dwindled to only two stallions

102

LEFT: This Dartmoor stallion is a pony that displays show quality, and others like it are regularly to be seen in ithe show ring, competing in mountain and moorland classes.

BELOW: The Dartmoor is an excellent child's pony, its small size making it easy to manage. It is also popular as a driving pony.

appear as bays and browns with only a little white on the legs and face. Height can be up to 12.2hh.

and 12 mares because of harsh winters spent without supplementary feeding. Nowadays the breed has been greatly improved and with careful monitoring is now flourishing. Children like to ride Dartmoors and they are also used for showing and driving.

The Dartmoor has a small, neat head, nicely set and with small, alert ears and intelligent and kindly eyes. The neck is of medium length and fairly well-developed, as are the back, loins and quarters. The tail is set high, the legs are shapely but sturdy, and the hooves are well-formed and hard.

Dartmoors make excellent children's ponies, and their small size makes them easily manageable. They also have kind and docile natures.

The Dartmoor's most striking feature is that it moves with almost no knee flexion, producing a long, free-flowing stride similar to that of a horse and very comfortable for the rider. They usually

DØLE GUDBRANDSDAL
(Norway)

The Døle Gudbrandsdal originated in the Gudbrandsdal valley, which is situated between the city of Oslo and the North Sea coast. Though much bigger, they are not dissimilar to the Dales and Fell ponies of Great Britain and it is thought that they share much of the same ancestry, namely the prehistoric Celtic Pony and the Friesian. This is feasible as the Friesian people are reputed to have traded all over Europe as well as in the British Isles and Scandinavia.

Over the centuries the Døle was crossed with other breeds, including Heavy Draft, Norfolk Trotter, Arab and Thoroughbred. The result was a horse that was strong and heavy enough for haulage as well as riding.

Today there is another Døle type: the original horse was extensively bred with Thoroughbreds to produce the Døle Trotter which is still used for trotting races in Norway.

The Second World War saw a depletion in numbers, but since 1962 efforts have been made to improve the quality of these horses by a breed society that will only register stallions with sound conformation and a good racetrack record. Døle's are still used on farms and are particularly useful in forestry work.

The Døle is the smallest of the draft horses and resembles a large pony. The head is small and neat with a broad forehead, straight or slightly Roman nose, and a square muzzle. The ears are small and alert and the eyes kind but inquisitive. The neck is short and well-developed with a slight crest. The chest and shoulders are very strong, the girth is deep, and the back is long with powerful, well-muscled hindquarters. The legs are short with plenty of good bone and feathering around the heels; the hooves are hard.

The Døle is a hardy breed, well able to withstand harsh winter conditions. It requires a modicum of care but can survive on little food. It is even-tempered and a willing worker.

Døles are usually bay, brown, chestnut or black, but occasionally grey or dun examples appear. The Trotter types often have white on their legs and faces. They are around 14.2–15.1hh.

DON (Russia)

The Don is Russia's most famous breed. It originated in the harsh Russian

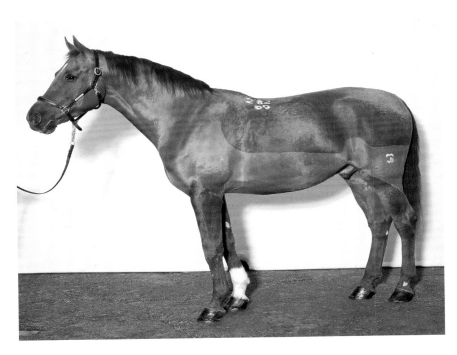

OPPOSITE & BELOW: The Don originated in the harsh conditions of the Russian steppes; consequently it is able to withstand extremes of temperature.

steppes, where it once roamed in herds, surviving the freezing winters and torrid summers with nothing but sparse vegetation for food.

The original steppes breed, known as the Old Don, was bred with various Orientals, such as Arabs, Karabakhs and Turkmenes, and Orlovs and Thoroughbreds were added to improve the Don's conformation and give it incredible stamina.

The horse was the preferred mount of the Don Cossacks; it was also used by the Russian army, and its extreme toughness made it an excellent hunter, particularly in pursuit of wolves. Today, the Don's hardy constitution makes it an excellent endurance horse. It is also used to improve other breeds.

The overall picture of the Don is one of strength and robustness. The head is fairly small and neat with a slightly dished or straight nose which clearly indicates its Arabian heritage. Ears are small and shapely and the eyes are large and intelligent. The neck is set high and should be arched; however, many have ewe necks. The back is fairly long,

straight and wide with sloping quarters and straight shoulders. The legs are clean but in some cases may be sickle-hocked. Moreover, the placement of the pelvis restricts movement and causes a stilted action (this fault had largely been bred out). Hooves are well-shaped and hard.

Dons are tough and sturdy with independent natures, qualities which have found their way into other breeds.

A striking feature of the coat is its iridescent sheen, this being most commonly chestnut but can also be bay, brown, black or grey. Height is 15.2hh.

DUTCH HEAVY DRAFT
(Netherlands)

The modern Dutch Draft is a relatively new breed, registered in the early 20th century when the Royal Association of the Netherlands Draft Horse was formed. Documentation of a heavy draft horse has existed since around 1850, however, while Holland and Belgium have had heavy horses for centuries, most notably the Brabant and Ardennais, whose history is very ancient.

These horses were crucial to the prosperity of the farming community, where their strength and massive feet made them capable of working heavy soil. It was these two breeds, along with native Zeeland-type mares, that created the Dutch Draft, the purity of which has long been protected by allowing entry to the stud book only to registered parents.

The Dutch Draft is an enormous horse for its height and is still used for heavy work on farms and for pulling brewers' drays. It can also be seen in the show ring.

The horse's head is large and square but also quite attractive, with a flat forehead and small but gentle eyes. The

The Dutch Heavy Draft was popular with farmers, who used the horse to till the soil and for hauling heavy loads.

ears are small and straight, the nose is straight, and the nostrils are large and flared. The neck is short and well-developed, while the body is short and deep and massively strong. The legs

resemble tree trunks, and abundant feathering is present on the legs.

The Dutch Draft is agile for its size, and it has a very lively gait. It usually has a long working life and is

tough, intelligent, kind, willing, and immensely strong.

Coats are predominantly chestnut and bay, but grey and black sometimes occur. Height is up to 17hh.

DUTCH WARMBLOOD

(Netherlands)

The Dutch Warmblood is a relatively new breed, its stud book having been opened in the Netherlands in 1958. It is enjoying huge success in showjumping and dressage and is in demand worldwide as a top-class competition horse.

The Dutch Warmblood differs from most European warmbloods in that it is based on no breed which existed in a slightly different form in previous centuries, and which has been improved, but contains breeds from all over Europe. The bases of the Dutch Warmblood are the Gelderlander and the heavier

The Dutch Warmblood is probably the most celebrated of the warmblood sports horses, excelling in competition year after year.

Groningen, which have been in existence in the Netherlands since the Middle Ages. The breeds themselves consist of many European strains, the Gelderlander being

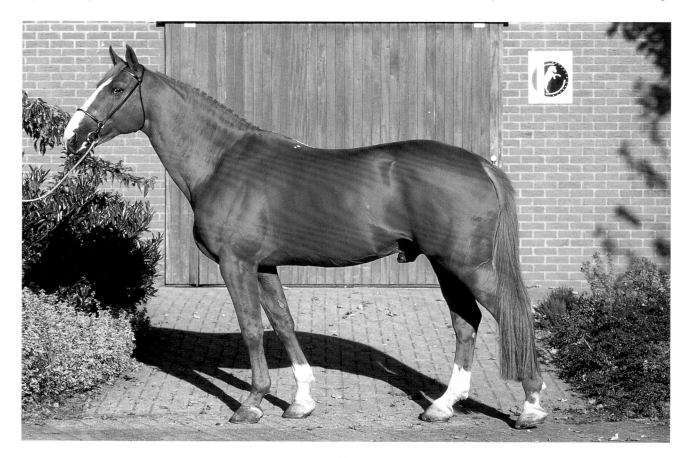

The Dutch Warmblood is lighter than many warmbloods. The head is attractive, the large, lively eyes look lively and alert, and the pricked ears are of medium size. The neck is well-set, long and muscular. The withers are prominent and the back is short and straight with powerful, slightly sloping quarters and a high-set tail. The shoulders are sloping and the legs are long and well-developed, ending in strong, shapely hooves.

The horse is renowned for its extravagant and elastic paces which make it such a competent performer at dressage and showjumping. It also has a sensible attitude to work with enough spark to perform the actions required of it. Its equable nature makes it amenable, a boon

LEFT: Dutch Warmbloods are particularly good at dressage. Here is Ferro, ridden by Corby van Baalen of the Netherlands, executing a piaffe at the 2000 Olympics.

BELOW: A Dutch Warmblood mare and foal at stud in the Netherlands.

a combination of Andalusian, Norman, Oldenburg, Hackney and Thoroughbred, to name but a few. The Groningen was created from Friesian and Oldenburg stock, which was chosen to produce correct conformation, good paces, and a strong presence, while a kind and willing nature and a certain amount of hardiness were also valuable traits.

Initially, the Dutch Warmblood was created by mating these two, with Thoroughbred added later to correct remaining conformation faults. The result was a little temperamental in character; to improve this, Hanoverian and Selle Français were added for level-headedness and acquiescence.

for the less experienced, and its flowing action makes it comfortable to ride.

Most commonly bay, chestnuts, greys and blacks are also possible. Height is 16hh and over.

EAST BULGARIAN (Bulgaria)

The East Bulgarian is unusual in that it contains no native Bulgarian foundation

stock, unlike most European warmbloods and other performance horses, which have combinations of native and Thoroughbred in their make-up. It was the Bulgarians' intention to create a horse which had excellent conformation, stamina, and endurance, and which could be used as a riding and light draft horse as well as in competition and performance work.

The breed came into existence at the end of the 19th century when the Kaiuk and Vassil Kolarov studs began a breeding programme, using Thoroughbreds and Thoroughbred crosses from Britain as well as Arabs and Anglo-Arabs. The established breed was similar to a middleweight Thoroughbred, which was further improved with more Thoroughbred blood. Now that the breed is truly established, mating occurs largely within the breed.

The East Bulgarian is a fine horse and its quality is immediately apparent. Today, it is used for general riding and competition, either ridden or in harness.

The head is fine, proud and noble, with a straight nose tapering to a neat muzzle with large, flared nostrils. The ears are medium-length and alert, the eyes expressive and lively, and the neck long and well-set. The body is similar to the Thoroughbred's, with sloping shoulders and a broad and deep chest and girth. It has well-developed hindquarters and

loins, its well-muscled upper legs being fine and long. The hooves are strong and well-shaped.

The East Bulgarian is beautifully made – proud, poised and elegant. Its stride is long and supple with all the speed, stamina and endurance of the pure-bred Thoroughbred and Arab. Although spirited and keen, it is also good-natured and willing to work.

Coats are most commonly chestnut or black, but occasionally bay and brown and very rarely grey can appear. The horses are smaller than most warmbloods, standing between 15 and 16hh.

EAST FRIESIAN (Germany)

For 300 years the East Friesian and the Oldenburg were regarded as the same breed, both having sprung from the same foundation stock. The two finally split with the division of Germany into East and West (the Oldenburg in the West) after the Second World War. Both the Oldenburg and the East Friesian are composed of Friesian, English half-bred, Oriental, Thoroughbred, Cleveland Bay, and Yorkshire Coach Horse, following which the breeds began to differ.

The breeders of Eastern Europe favoured lighter horses that were more Oriental in appearance, so as well as adding horses from Poland and France, they also turned to Arabs. They consulted

the Babolna Stud in Hungary, which is the oldest and most respected in Europe, from whence they took Arab stallions and in particular the famous stallion Gazal, which played an important part in the improvement of the breed. The East Friesian had by now changed so much that it bore little resemblance to its brother, the Oldenburg. In latter years, lighter Hanoverians have also been added to make the horse more suitable for performance and competition.

The East Friesian's head is fine and wedge-shaped and similar to that of the Arab; it has medium-length pointed ears, kind and intelligent eyes, and a straight nose. The neck is long and elegant, set on nicely sloping shoulders. The chest and girth are deep. The body is medium-length with strong loins and well-developed hindquarters. The legs are long and strong.

This is a quality sports horse with boundless energy, stamina and endurance. It has a spirited but kindly nature and is always eager to work. It requires the same care as any other fine-quality horse in the form of winter shelter and a regimen of feeding and exercise.

Coats come in most solid colours and grey, but there can be white on the face and lower legs. Height is 15.2–16.1hh.

ERISKAY (U.K.)

The history of the Eriskay is an ancient one, it being a true native breed with Celtic and Norse connections. The ponies once roamed all over the Western Isles of Scotland, where they were caught and used as work ponies to carry seaweed and peat in panniers laid across their backs – also in harness. They were not only strong but also hardy, and were able to survive on the sparse vegetation that was the only food available.

The menfolk were fishermen and spent most of their time at sea, leaving the ponies mainly in the care of the women and children. By the 19th century, however, mechanization was causing a dramatic depletion in their numbers with only a few ponies remaining. By the 1970s only a handful were left living on the isle of Eriskay, situated between South Uist and Barra. This is how the pony got its name and which is where it remained undisturbed, with no other stock to dilute the bloodline, thus keeping the breed pure. The Eriskay is still counted a Category 1 pony on the rare breed list and is in fact still Britain's rarest breed.

Today, with the introduction of breeding programmes, numbers are on the increase and Eriskays are proving popular in many children's riding activities, including pony club events, showjumping and eventing. They are also successful as

driving ponies, with harnessed pairs excelling at high levels of competition.

The head is fairly plain and workmanlike, with bold eyes spaced well apart in a wide forehead. The ears are small and the nose straight with a tapering muzzle; the expression is inquisitive. The neck is set high and proud, with sloping shoulders and a deep chest. The body is short and strong with well-developed quarters and a low-set tail. The legs are fine, with a little feathering on the fetlocks, and small hard hooves. The coat is very dense, but not particularly long, and it is waterproof to protect it from the harsh environment.

The Eriskay makes an excellent family pony. It is good-natured, easy to handle, and needs little looking after; indeed, it will happily live out all year round. Eriskays thrive on human companionship and seem to like children in particular. Nevertheless, they are very

The Eriskay is Britain's rarest breed and is the subject of a programme to preserve it and keep it pure. Small herds of Eriskays can still be seen on the small island, situated between South Uist and Barra.

strong and despite their small size will carry an adult with ease.

These ponies are usually grey but foals are born black or bay and lighten as they mature. No other colours are possible. Height is 12–13.2hh.

EXMOOR (U.K.)

The Exmoor is truly ancient, said to have existed before the last Ice Age when similar ponies migrated south from Alaska, and where bones that match those of the modern pony have been found. Exmoor's isolated position, covering remote areas of the counties of Devon and Somerset, has ensured that very little cross-breeding has occurred, which has maintained the purity of the breed; indeed, the Exmoor pony is one of the purest breeds in the world, unlike its cousin, the Dartmoor, which is more accessible and has consequently gone through many changes.

Exmoors are truly wild ponies and still live up on the moors, though today they are closely monitored, being regarded as a rare breed with only 1,000 ponies worldwide. In the United Kingdom there are aproximately 300 breeding mares which produce around 130 foals a year. Half of these mares still live on Exmoor and to protect the purity of the breed each foal is inspected, numbered, and branded on its flank, with the society's mark and herd number on the shoulder.

There are also various farms in the area which are involved with the breeding of Exmoors, with the result that its future is now looking rather brighter. Nowadays Exmoors are also being bred in other parts of Britain, but all still use the moor

The ancient Exmoor breed is now rare, with only 1,000 ponies existing worldwide. There are still herds living wild up on the moors, and these are closely monitored to keep the breed pure and ensure its survival.

ponies as their foundation stock to ensure the purity of the breed. Ponies which have been broken are used for children's riding events as well as for driving classes.

The head is large with a broad forehead and hooded eyes to protect the pony from the elements: this is known as 'toad-eyed'. The ears are thick and short and the nose straight. The neck is thick and well-developed, with a deep chest; the short, fine legs are nevertheless muscular and strong, with a little feathering around the fetlocks. The hooves are small and hard. The coat is dense, with a thick, wiry mane and tail.

Exmoors are extremely tough and can live out all year round. If they are to be domesticated, they must be caught and broken in while young. They are good-natured, willing and obedient and make good children's ponies.

Coats are bay, brown or dun with black points. There should be the distinctive mealy markings around the eyes, muzzle and flanks, but with no white whatsoever. Mares should not exceed 12.2hh or stallions 12.3hh.

FALABELLA (Argentina)

The Falabella was created a century ago by the Falabella family at their ranch near Buenos Aires in Argentina. The breed was established by crossing small Thoroughbred and Arab stallions with Shetland Pony mares; then, using selective inbreeding, the Falabella became smaller and smaller to produce the breed as we know it today.

The Falabella is not a pony: it is a miniature horse with all the conformation and character of a horse. However, the conformation of some is not ideal, due to too much inbreeding, and they can consequently look rather odd; moreover, they are weak for their size and can only be ridden by the very smallest children. Today, breeders are attempting to rectify these faults and are generally trying to improve the breed.

Falabellas make ideal pets, being most affectionate, and because of their small size are even allowed into peoples' homes. They should be given the same level of care as a Thoroughbred.

Although they cannot be ridden, Falabellas are popular in specially allocated in-hand showing classes and are capable of pulling small carts.

A Fallabella should resemble a miniature Thoroughbred or Arab, if correctly bred, though some specimens show evidence of their Shetland ancestry. The head is refined and horse-like, with a straight nose and small, flared nostrils. The small ears are wide apart, and the eyes are kind. The body is medium-length, with a slim frame, and the fine legs resemble those of a Thoroughbred.

This is a delightful breed that provides all the pleasures of a larger breed at a much reduced cost as far as land requirements are concerned. Its constitution is less than robust, however, and it requires the same care that one would give to any finely bred horse. It is amenable, docile and obedient.

Falabellas come in all solid colours as well as grey and roan. Appaloosa markings are also common.

They should be no taller than 30in (76cm).

Falabellas are regarded as small horses rather than ponies. They make affectionate pets, even though they are too small and weak to ride except by the smallest children. They are capable, however, of pulling very small carts.

FELL (U.K.)

The Fell is closely related to the Dales pony, though it originated on the western side of the Pennines. It is a descendant of the Celtic Pony which once roamed much of northern Europe, and which the Romans used as draft animals and in raids against the Picts. They were later used by reivers – the cattle-raiders of the Scottish Border country – who required ponies with strength, stamina and sure-footedness.

The Fells' chequered history continued when they were used by smugglers around the northern coastlines, and they were also bred by Cistercian monks who introduced grey ponies, as white stock signified monastic ownership. Over the years, and like the Dales, the breed was improved by matings with other stock, such as the Friesian, to which the Fell bears a strong resemblance. However, it remains much purer then the Dales which has been subjected to rather more added bloodstock.

Like many native breeds, numbers declined during and after the two World Wars, when farms switched to machinery and motorized transport as they became more readily available. However, the Fell remained popular as a riding and driving pony and its fortunes have happily been reversed. Today, the Fell is an all-round family pony, strong enough to carry an adult and sufficiently docile for children to ride. They make excellent trekking ponies and are therefore popular with the tourist industry. They are also used in harness and the occasional farmer still uses them to herd sheep.

The Fell bears a strong resemblance to the Friesian. The head is noble with a broad forehead and a straight or slightly dished, tapering nose with large flared nostrils. The eyes are proud and intelligent and the ears small and neat. The head sits well on the neck, which is of medium length, strong, but not overdeveloped. The shoulders are well-muscled and sloping, ensuring a good

smooth action. The body is sturdy with a strong back and a deep chest. The legs are strong and muscular with fine feathering present on the backs of the legs; the hooves are well-shaped and are a characteristic blue colour. Mane and tail should not be trimmed but should be left to grow naturally.

The Fell has an excellent constitution, and like most mountain and moorland ponies is hardy and able to live out all year round. It is easy-going and enjoys the company of humans beings; however, it is a free spirit and can be wilful at times. Fell ponies are famous for their excellent paces, which make them comfortable to ride. They excel at endurance events and are fast into the bargain, which is an asset in harness.

A pure black coat with no white markings is the most popular, but bays, greys and browns are also possible, when a small amount of white is permissible in the form of a small star on the forehead or a little around the fetlocks. Height is up to 14hh.

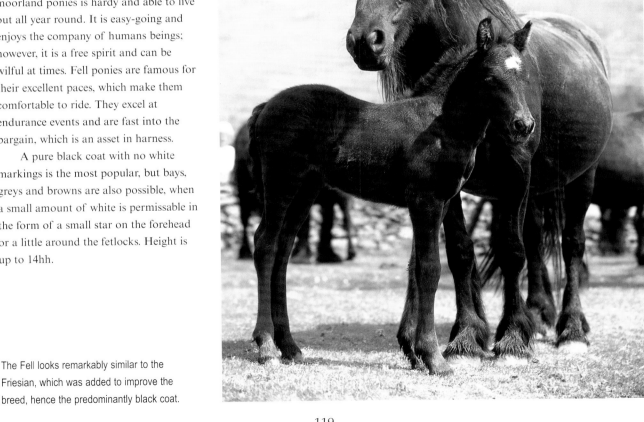

The Fell looks remarkably similar to the Friesian, which was added to improve the breed, hence the predominantly black coat.

FJORD (Norway)

It is likely that the Fjord is descended from the Przewalski or Asiatic Wild Horse, which in turn is descended from the horses of the last Ice Age. It seems to have retained much of its ancestors' characteristics, for example, the pale coat, dorsal stripe down the back, and occasional zebra stripes on the legs, typical of the ancient breed. The primitive breed was improved over many hundreds of years by breeding with the Celtic Pony and the Tarpan. The result has been in use for thousands of years, and there is evidence that it was utilized in raids and battles, as evidenced by Viking artifacts. The Vikings had a particularly bloodthirsty approach to selection in which they allowed stallions to fight to the death, when the victor became the breeding stallion.

The breed still has its mane clipped in the fashion to be seen on Viking rune stones; the mane is unusual in that it is cream on the outer edges and black in the centre, being part of the dorsal stripe. The mane is therefore clipped so that the black part is prominent.

The Fjord has been used to improve many other northern European breeds, including the Icelandic and Highland. Today it can be seen over most of Scandinavia, mainly used as children's riding ponies. It is sure-footed and excellent at trekking and long-distance

endurance events. It is also popular in harness, where it has been successful in competition. Some are still used around farms for light ploughing and as useful packhorses.

The head is attractive, being short and wide with short, neat ears, a slightly dished face, and large nostrils. The eyes are large and kind. The neck is short and thick, accentuated by the clipped mane, a

tradition which has survived since ancient times. The body is sturdy, with sloping quarters and a low-set tail. The legs are strong, with plenty of good bone, and the feet are tough and hard.

The Fjord's most striking features are its dorsal stripe and primitive appearance.

Coats are usually a pale gold or dun colour, with a black dorsal stripe running from the poll to the tail; this also runs

The Fjord is most likely the descendant of the Przewalski or Asiatic Wild Horse, on account of the characteristic dorsal stripe that runs from poll to tail.

through the centre of the mane, the outer sections of which are white. Some also have zebra stripes on the legs. Height is 13.2–14.2hh.

FREDERIKSBORG (Denmark)

The Frederiksborg's history is long, stretching back to the mid-1500s when the Royal Frederiksborg Stud was founded. The aim of the stud was to breed a horse for the classical *haute école* method of training, which reached a peak of popularity in the 19th century. The breed is based on small, native Danish and Jutland Draft mares which were bred with Andalusian and Neapolitan stallions. These were then mixed with Turkish and Dutch breeds as well as Thoroughbreds.

The Frederiksborg made its name as a warhorse and also as a carriage horse. Because it was in such demand, however, many were sold abroad which dramatically depleted the stock; this was further aggravated by the closure of the stud in 1862. Some stock survived in the hands of private breeders and the Frederiksborg was then further improved to bring it up to modern competition standards by breeding it with Oldenburg, Friesian, Arab, and Thoroughbred. Today it is used mainly as a general riding horse and also in harness, though it can still be seen around farms. It

The Frederiksborg was bred mainly for the cavalry and also as a carriage horse, though today it is used for general riding. Frederiksborg stock was also used to produce the excellent Danish Warmblood.

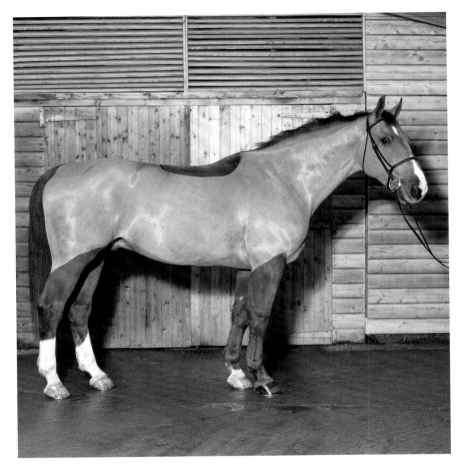

is interesting to note that Frederiksborg-Thoroughbred stock was the basis of the rather more popular Danish Warmblood.

The Frederiksborg has all the characteristics of a warmblood. The head is fairly broad with a straight nose, intelligent eyes, and alert medium-length ears. The neck is thick but carried high and proud. The body is of medium length with a good strong shoulder and a deep chest. The legs are long and well-developed.

This is an excellent all-rounder, possessing strength, stamina and an equable disposition. The Frederiksborg is particularly well known for its trot, which is high-stepping and floating. Coats are usually chestnut. Height is 15.1–16.1hh.

FRENCH ANGLO-ARAB
(France)

The Anglo-Arab derives its name from two of the world's greatest breeds, the Thoroughbred, which is of English (Anglo) origin and the Arabian. The rule governing Anglo-Arab breeding is very strict in the United Kingdom, and only these two breeds can be present. As this is not a standardized breed, however, the resulting progeny can either resemble the Thoroughbred, the Arab, or a little of both.

The French Anglo-Arab is different in that it is a composite breed, developed in the 1830s by a veterinary surgeon by the name of Gayot. It was later mixed with the bloodlines of two stallions, an Arab called Massoud and a Turk called Aslan, together with those of three Thoroughbred mares.

Today the breeding of a French Anglo-Arab consists of pure-bred Arab, Anglo-Arab, and Thoroughbred. To register a French Anglo-Arab in the stud book the horse must have at least 25 per cent Arab and no other blood other then Arab and Thoroughbred going back six generations. The French Anglo-Arab

excels in all disciplines, including racing and endurance.

This horse exudes quality. The head is small and fine with either a straight or sightly dished nose and a tapering muzzle with fine expressive nostrils. The eyes are kind and intelligent and the ears medium-length, well-shaped and alert. The head is carried high and sits well on a long shapely neck; the body is medium-length and sinewy with a deep girth and sloping shoulders. The legs are long and fine but strong.

The French Anglo-Arab exudes quality and combines all the excellent traits of the Arabian and Thoroughbred.

This horse combines the Arab's intelligence and beauty with the Thoroughbred's size and speed.

Chestnut is the most common; however, all solid colours are acceptable, with white allowed on the legs and face. Height is 15.2–16.3hh.

FRENCH TROTTER (France)

The first trotting racetrack in France opened in 1839 at Cherbourg and since that date the sport has not looked back. The first races were a means of selecting suitable stallions and became quite an event. The most popular trotters at that time were Norman and Anglo-Norman breeds; later, these were crossed with Norfolk Roadsters from Britain and by the end of the 19th century the breed had been further enhanced by infusions of British Hackney, Orlov Trotter from Russia, and Thoroughbred. These breeds did much to create a popular and much respected trotter, and with the later addition of American Standardbred, which greatly improved the breed, it was considered complete.

In 1906 a stud book was created for French Trotters, though the breed itself wasn't recognized as such until 1922. To be acceptable for registration it was necessary that the horse be able to trot a

distance of 0.62 mile (1km) in 1 minute 42 seconds. This was later extended to include only horses whose parents had both been registered, thus ensuring the purity of the breed. Recently, however, further infusions of Standardbreds have been made to improve the breed and its paces, the result being a world-class trotting horse which even surpasses the Standardbred itself.

Today it is predominantly used for the sport for which it was bred, both under saddle and in harness; but French Trotters also make good riding horses and even capable jumpers. The horses which have been bred for riding have also been used to sire competition horses, particularly the Selle Français.

In appearance, the French Trotter's Thoroughbred ancestry is much in evidence, and includes a noble head, broad forehead, medium-sized far-apart ears, and kind, intelligent eyes. The nostrils are large and flaring. The neck is long and well-developed, with a straight shoulder, deep chest, and well-formed, powerful quarters. Legs are muscular with plenty of bone and well-shaped hooves.

The French Trotter has all the fine characteristics of the Thoroughbred, with the noble head and fine conformation that exudes quality.

The French Trotter has a good turn of speed, plenty of stamina, and an even temperament, though it is not without spirit. The harness horses are usually a little smaller and lighter than ridden types.

Like the Thoroughbred, all solid coat colours are available, and there is the occasional roan. Greys are quite rare. Height is approximately 16.2hh.

FRIESIAN (Netherlands)

The Friesian is the Netherland's only surviving indigenous breed and is descended from a native breed which roamed Friesland, the western part of the ancient region of Frisia, 3,000 years ago, and where the remains of a similar coldblooded horse have been found. As riding horses, the Friesian's history is an ancient one, with evidence that they were used by Roman soldiers when they were building Hadrian's Wall in around 150 AD; this is also supported by the fact that Fell and Dales breeds native to the Pennines are also descended from Friesians. Friesian blood is also present in the Orlov Trotter as well as in most American trotters.

Over the years the original breed, which was rather heavy and plain, was infused with Oriental and Andalusian blood, which improved it to such as extent that during the 17th century Friesians were seen along with Spanish horses performing *haute école*, and were in demand as elegant carriage horses. During the 19th century, however, the Friesian became a rarity, the breed being almost exclusively restricted to Friesland, where it was used as a general riding horse and trotter. By the end of the First World War the Friesian was in dire peril of extinction, with only three stallions and a few mares still in existence. Thankfully, with careful breeding and an infusion of Oldenburg blood, the Friesian is once again flourishing; today, it is in evidence all over the world, much admired for its noble presence and expressive trot, which is particularly striking in harness. It is still used in *haute école* disciplines.

The head is proud and of medium size with small, alert ears which point sightly inwards. The eyes are kindly and expressive. The head-carriage is high and elegant, and the neck is of medium length

Traditionally the Friesian is quite a small horse, usually standing at about 15.2hh; however, with its popularity as a dressage horse increasing, it is now being bred larger, and can attain 16hh.

with a high crest. The withers are well-developed, tapering into the back muscles, and the shoulders sloping. The back is of medium length, strong and straight, leading to well-developed loins and quarters. The legs are clean and strong, with slight feathering, and the mane and tail long and luxuriant; when showing,

mane and tail should be left untrimmed.

The Friesian has a proud bearing but is nevertheless gentle and amenable if rather energetic. Black, with only the smallest of white stars on the face, is the only colour permitted. Height is 15–15.2hh, but some Friesians have been bred larger, attaining over 16hh.

FURIOSO (Hungary)

As a breed, the Furioso has only existed for about 150 years. It was developed by Hungary's famous Mezőhegyes Stud, which was founded by the Habsburg Emperor Joseph II in 1785, and where the Nonius was also bred.

In 1840 the stud imported an English Thoroughbred called Furioso, and in 1843 another, North Star, which was a Norfolk Roadster. They mated these two with Nonius and Arab mares, the result being two very distinctive breeds, the Furioso and the North Star. By 1885, however, the two breeds had merged to such an extent that only one breed remained, with Furioso traits predominating.

Today the Furioso is in use as an all-round riding horse and it is also an excellent jumper. It has plenty of stamina, which makes it a competent steeplechaser.

The Furioso is a quality horse, possessing all the attributes of its Thoroughbred forebears. The head is fine, with a straight nose leading to a squarish muzzle. The ears are medium-length and shapely. The eyes are inquisitive and bold. The neck is long and elegant with fine sloping shoulders; the girth is deep and the legs are long and strong. The quarters are well-developed with a high tail-carriage.

Most noticeable is the action of the high-stepping knee, which is inherited

BELOW: A herd of Furioso horses at stud in Hungary.

OPPOSITE: The Furioso is a fine-quality horse with many of the attributes of its Thoroughbred forebears.

from the Nonius. The Furioso makes an elegant carriage horse as well as a riding horse; it has all the amenability of the Thoroughbred, together with its spirit and courage.

Furiosos are usually brown, black or bay, with only minimal white markings. Height is approximately 16.1hh.

GALICEÑO (Mexico)

The first horses to arrive in the Americas came with the Spanish conquistadors in the 16th century. Many either escaped or became the property of the native population, eventually becoming almost indigenous to the continent. The Galiceño is descended from the Garrano mountain ponies of Portugal and Galician horses from north-west Spain, said to have come to Mexico with Cortez. Though used by the Mexicans, they were also allowed to roam in a semi-wild state, where the breed developed by means of natural selection.

The Galiceño has much Arab blood in its make-up and has inherited many of the characteristics of the breed, in looks as well as stamina. Galiceños are popular in North America as children's riding ponies and do well in children's competitions. In Latin America they are still used for work on ranches, where strength and stamina is important; in fact, the Galiceño is capable of carrying a man over rugged terrain for an entire day without tiring. It has an ususual gait, known as a 'running walk', which enables it to cover ground quickly, efficiently and smoothly, making it ideal for riding and when it is in harness.

The Galiceño is small and compact, its Arab ancestry apparent in the head, which is fine and narrow, with thin pointed ears, a small muzzle, and large, flared nostrils. The eyes are large and intelligent. The neck is long and well- developed with a long, full mane. The withers are prominent with a good sloping shoulder and a deep girth. The body is quite stocky, but the back is unusually narrow. Unlike the Arab, the tail is set low and, like the mane, is allowed to grow long. The legs are fine but very strong, with well-shaped, hard hooves.

The Galiceño is well-known for its toughness, stamina and ability to travel long distances without tiring. It is comfortable to ride because of its long, smooth gait. Its intelligence and quick reactions make it an excellent competitor.

All the usual solid colours, including palomino, dun and grey are present. Part-coloureds or albinos are not permitted. Height is 12–13.2hh.

The Galiceño, of Iberian origin, is strong and hardy, able to carry a man all day over long distances without tiring. It has an unusual gait, known as a 'running walk'.

wide range of tasks, for haulage, in the army, for general agriculture, forestry and trekking, and as a packhorse.

This lightweight pony owes much of its appearance to its Oriental ancestors, though the conformation of the primitive pony is still in evidence. The head is small and fine with a slightly dished face. The back is short and the hindquarters underdeveloped. The shoulders are rather straight, but the legs are fine and well-muscled, ending in strong, neat hooves.

The Garrano is Portugal's oldest breed, dating back to prehistoric times. It is a versatile animal and is useful in many tasks.

There is a shaggy mane and tail.

They are tough and hardy, Garranos require little care. They have great strength and stamina with plenty of energy and are good-natured and amenable. They are bay or dark chestnut. Their height is up to 14hh.

GARRANO (Portugal)

The Garrano, the 'little horse' of Portugal, is an ancient breed, its origins dating to prehistoric times. It comes from the Minho and Tras-os-Montes areas of northern Portugal, and was probably bred with Oriental horses, such as Barbs and Arabs, which were brought to the Iberian peninsula during the Moorish occupation of the 8th century. These greatly improved conformation and the Garrano's ability to work and be ridden. The pony is used for a

GELDERLANDER (Netherlands)

The Gelderlander, or Gelderland, is a warmblood which originated in the province of Gelder in the Netherlands. The breed was created by Dutch farmers who required an all-round workhorse for their own use, as well as an animal they could sell on as a good-quality riding and carriage horse. In fact, the Gelderlander has been used by many royal houses throughout Europe to draw carriages on state ceremonial occasions.

Native heavy mares from the Gelder were bred with Andalusian, Neapolitan, Norman, Norfolk Roadster and Holstein stallions to produce a well-built horse. In the 19th century the breed was further improved when East Friesian, Oldenburg, Hackney and Thoroughbred were introduced. Today the horse is an excellent all-rounder, with a talent for showjumping; its high-stepping action is presumably inherited from its trotter forebears. The Gelderland appears in the

ancestry of other modern warmbloods, notably the Dutch Warmblood, which was established as a breed in the late 1950s. Nowadays there are very few Gelderlanders as the Dutch Warmblood has overtaken them in popularity. However, there are a few interested persons who strive to keep the old breed alive.

The horse has a plain but well-porportioned head with a straight or slightly Roman nose. The ears are fine,

shapely and expressive, and the eyes are kind. The neck is fairly long and muscular, with a slightly pronounced crest. The withers are prominent and the back is long and straight with a short croup and a high-set tail. The girth is deep with a long sloping shoulder, strong, muscular legs and large, tough hooves.

The Gelderlander has a charming, easy-going disposition and is a willing worker. It is a good all-rounder, equally at home jumping or as part of a team pulling a carriage. Most common are chestnuts, but blacks, bays or greys are also seen. There is a good deal of white on the head and legs. Height is 15.2–16.2hh.

The Gelderlander was originally bred as an all-rounder, to work on farms and as a riding and carriage horse. Today, however, it has lost much of its popularity to the Dutch Warmblood, but fortunately there are still people interested enough to ensure that the breed continues.

GIDRÁN (Hungary)

The Gidrán was developed at the Mezöhegyes State Stud, which was founded by the Habsburg Emperor Joseph II in 1785. This important Hungarian breeding establishment was also responsible for the development of the Nonius in the early 19th century and the Furioso from 1885. In about 1816, however, the Hungarians had required a cavalry horse, with all the stamina, strength and courage of the Arab, albeit in a larger form. Consequently, another breed, the Hungarian Anglo-Arab, or Gidrán, had also been developed.

The creation of the Gidrán was complicated in that there were more varied bloodlines in its composition than the traditional Anglo-Arab, with its varying amounts of Arab and Thoroughbred. The stud imported an Arab stallion, said to have come from the Siglavi (Seglawy) strain, and called Gidrán Senior, which was mated with various breeds of mare, such as Arab, Turkish and Spanish-Naples. From these unions seven colts were born which became Mezöhegyes's premier stallions.

In 1820 the Spanish-Naples mare, Arrogante, gave birth to a colt which was named Gidrán II, and which became the foundation stallion of the breed; today all Gidráns can be traced to this one stallion. The breed was further developed using

Arab, Transylvanian, Spanish, Nonius and native Hungarian horses, and by 1893 Thoroughbred blood was added to further improve the breed – also Shagya Arabs Gazal III and Siglavy II, which added more Arabian attributes to the breed. The end result was a horse that was very fast, was a good jumper, and had excellent stamina.

Nowadays the Gidrán is used for competition riding and driving, and its excellent breeding makes it suitable for

The superb Gidrán has all the attributes of the Anglo-Arab, allied with enormous presence and elegance. This horse is shown at the famous Mezöhegyes State Stud in Hungary, where the breed was developed.

improving other breeds. However, it is now extremely rare, with less than 200 examples left in the world, placing it in very real danger of extinction.

The Gidrán has all the excellent qualities of the Anglo-Arab. It has a fine intelligent head, with a straight or slightly dished face, fine alert ears, and an inquisitive look. The neck is long and beautifully shaped. The body is strong, sturdy and muscular with long, straight legs. The quarters are powerful, as with all horses capable of attaining great speeds.

All the qualities of the horse's noble ancestry are immediately apparent, allied with a strong impression of strength, power and vigour. The Gidrán has great courage and will-power which, coupled with agility and intelligence, makes it an excellent competition horse.

Usually chestnuts, the horses stand at 16.1–17hh.

GOTLAND (Sweden)

The Gotland, or Skogruss, the 'little horse of the woods', is an ancient breed, said to be directly descended from the wild Tarpan, and has lived on the island of Gotland in the Baltic Sea for 4–5,000 years, and probably much longer. Because of its isolation, and the commitment of the local inhabitants to keep the breed intact, there has been little or no cross-breeding, and the Gotland has remained largely true to type. The Russ, as some of the locals call it, still lives on the wooded wild moors of the island to this day.

Gotlands were also kept on the mainland, where in 1886 the breed was improved with a Syrian stallion; consequently, their blood is not as pure as their island cousins. For centuries they worked on local farms and also became popular in other European countries, where they were exported for use in light haulage and also in mines. Like many native breeds, numbers declined rapidly with the onset of mechanization in the early 1900s. In the 1950s, however, the continuity of the breed was assured when the Swedish Pony Association was formed, set up by the government to protect this unusual and attractive breed, which was further improved using two Welsh stallions. Today the breed is flourishing and is used in trotting races and as a general children's riding pony, at which it excels.

The head is medium-sized with a broad forehead, small pricked ears, a straight nose, and large, clever eyes. The neck is medium-length and well-developed, with prominent withers; the back is straight with sloping hindquarters. The full tail is low-set, and the legs are fine but very strong, with small, well-shaped hard feet.

The Gotland is robust and long-lived, with many surviving into their 30s; they are energetic, intelligent and friendly, and make excellent first mounts.

They are usually black, bay, dun or chestnut. Some have a dorsal stripe, indicative of their primitive origins. They stand around 11.2–13.2hh.

GRONINGEN (Netherlands)

The Groningen's bloodline has been of vital importance in the breeding of modern warmbloods in the Netherlands, the prototype being an old Dutch breed which originated in the north-eastern province of Groningen; it was bred for use as a heavyweight riding horse as well as for general farm use.

The breed was established by crossing East Friesian and German Oldenburg with the native stock of the area. A heavier horse was needed to farm the heavy soil of the region, so Suffolk Punch and Norfolk Roadster stallions were also introduced to make the Groningen a more substantial animal than its near neighbour, the Gelderlander, which came from a region of lighter soil. Both horses are the foundation of the now internationally famous Dutch Warmblood, and the powerful well-developed quarters of the Groningen can clearly be seen in the new breed, which is an excellent showjumper. Nowadays, however, the Groningen, along with the Gelderlander, is a rare breed.

The Groningen has a long, rather plain head with long ears and a docile expression. The neck is medium-length and well-developed, with prominent withers; the back is long, the croup flattened, and the tail set high, with very muscular quarters. The girth has plenty of depth and the legs are short and strong with plenty of bone. The hooves are well-shaped.

Good-natured and amenable, the Groningen has great strength, stamina and power – attributes which it has passed to the Dutch Warmblood. They are mainly black, brown and bay and stand at 15.3–16.1hh.

The Groningen, along with the Gelderlander, played an important part in the development of the Dutch Warmblood, and the strength and stamina of the Groningen can clearly be seen in the Dutch Warmblood's hindquarters.

HACKNEY (U.K.)

The Hackney breed first emerged in the 18th and 19th centuries in Norfolk and Yorkshire, where it was used by farmers who prized it for its stamina. A little later it came to be used for sport, particularly for trotting both in harness and under saddle, and was capable of amazing speeds: one mare, Nonpareil, was said to have trotted 100 miles (160km) in just under ten hours. But it was as a high-stepping carriage horse that the Hackney was principally known, making it indispensable until the 1920s when it was gradually replaced by the motor car.

The Hackney owes its trotting ability to its breeding: its probable foundation stock consisted of Norfolk and Yorkshire trotter which was bred with Arab and Thoroughbred blood for heightened performance. Hackney ponies are also derived from English trotters, with additions of Fell and Welsh Pony. Both Hackney horses and ponies have a registered stud book which was established in 1883.

Today the Hackney is underutilized, usually seen in the show ring, where its extravagant paces are demonstrated, harnessed to smart renovated carriages. But they are beginning to be seen in driving competitions and even dressage, showjumping and eventing. They are

also mated with other breeds to enhance the modern sports horse.

The head-carriage is high and proud, with fine, alert ears and intelligent eyes. The nose is straight or slightly Roman. The neck is long and well-developed, with a high crest leading to good sloping shoulders and a short-coupled body. The quarters are strong and powerful, and the legs are sturdy, furnished with plenty of bone.

Lively and fiery, the Hackney is most definitely not for the novice. It has enormous stamina and the ability to trot for many miles without tiring. It is best known for its extravagant action, where the front legs are brought up very high before being flung straight out from the shoulder.

The Hackney was bred in the 18th century as a carriage and riding horse. It is distinguished by its high-stepping gait, displayed to its full extent in the show ring.

Colours are mostly bay, brown and black; less commonly chestnut and roan. There is usually white on the head and face. Pony 12–14hh: horse 14.2–15.2hh.

HAFLINGER (Austria)

The history of the Haflinger is obscure and there are various opinions as to its true origins. It is thought to have come from the South Tyrol on the Austrian side of the border with Italy, though borders have changed many times throughout history, making the exact location impossible to pinpoint. The Haflinger, however, is not unlike the slightly larger Avelignese from the Italian side.

The Haflinger may have been the result of native stock breeding with Oriental horses, which were left behind when the Ostrogoths were driven north by the Byzantine forces in the 6th century. Another story is that King Louis IV of Germany gave a Burgundian stallion to his son as a wedding gift, which was mated with local mares of Oriental origin to produce the Haflinger breed; either way there is little doubt that Oriental blood is present.

But it is a definite fact that the modern Haflinger breed was improved in 1868, when the Arab stallion, El Bedavi XXII, was imported to the region and bred with Haflinger mares; today, all Haflingers are related to this one stallion.

The Arab blood can be clearly seen in the fine head, which is in sharp contrast with the stocky body. Nowadays, the Haflinger is still to be found in Austria, where it is closely monitored in government-organized breeding programmes, as well as by private individuals. The breed is also popular the world over, particularly in Europe, where it is used in the forests and farms of the Tyrol. It is useful in harness, and as a children's riding pony and family pet.

The Haflinger has a noble Arab head with a slightly dished nose, large, attentive eyes, small alert ears, and neat nostrils

and muzzle. The neck is well-proportioned, with fine sloping shoulders, good withers, and a deep girth. The body is broad and strong with muscular quarters and a high-set tail. The legs are of medium length with very strong, tough hooves.

The Haflinger is a sociable animal and enjoys the company of people. It is intelligent, trustworthy and docile, making it an excellent work pony as well as children's pet. Haflingers are hardy and require only moderate feeding; however, they do require shelter from cold winds and wet weather. Their most striking feature is their flaxen mane and tail.

Various shades of chestnut, liver or red are permitted, sometimes with a little dappling over paler areas. White patches are undesirable. The distinctive mane and tail are usually left long. Height is up to 14hh.

OPPOSITE: The Haflinger's most striking feature is its flaxen mane and tail.

ABOVE: Three Haflingers at the Fohlenhof Stud at Ebbs, Austria.

HANOVERIAN (Germany)

The Hanoverian has a long history, the earliest reference to it being in the 8th century when it was used at the Battle of Poitiers, in which Charles Martel stemmed the advance of the Saracens. These were heavy warhorses, probably a combination of native, Spanish and Oriental influences.

The horses owe their evolution to warfare, and by the Middle Ages developed to be large and cob-like, capable of carrying a knight clad in heavy armour. The type was favoured for many centuries, but changes in warfare techniques meant that a lighter horse was eventually required. At this time the Hanoverian was still a heavy breed, even though it was taller and more agile than the cob type; by the 17th century there were three distinctive types of horse bred for military purposes: the Hanoverian, Mecklenburg and Danish.

But it was in the 18th century that the Hanoverian truly came into its own, when a member of the House of Hanover, in the person of George I, ascended the British throne in 1714, but spent much of his reign in Hanover; for the next 100 years or so the Hanoverian was nurtured and improved. English Thoroughbred stallions

were bred with Hanoverian mares, and Cleveland Bay was also added to produce a horse that was still quite heavy and which was used for farm and coach work.

It was George II who established the state stud at Celle in 1735, where horses for agriculture, riding and driving were bred. Here the Hanoverian breed was improved still further with the addition of Thoroughbred and Trakehner blood; the Hanoverian breed registry was founded in 1888, the end result being a horse which is similar to the fabulous competition horse of today – probably the best known of all warmbloods – which excels the world over in top dressage and showjumping.

Nowadays, the Society of Breeders of the Hanoverian Warmblood Horse is responsible for the purity of the breed. Approximately 150–160, most of them stallions, are kept by the state and are based at Celle, where they are required to undergo tests for soundness, conformation and character for several months before they are allowed to mate.

The Hanoverian has played a large part in the improvement and formation of other warmblood breeds, such as the Westphalian, Mecklenburg and Brandenburg. Hanoverians now come in two types: the heavier ones are used for showjumping, while the lighter ones, which have more Thoroughbred blood, are used for dressage.

Near-perfect in conformation, the Hanoverian's Thoroughbred characteristics are immediately discernible. The head is of medium size, with a straight nose and keen, alert eyes and pricked ears. The neck makes a graceful arch and is long and muscular, while the chest is well-developed, with a deep girth and sloping shoulder. The back is of medium length, with muscular loins and powerful quarters. The legs are strong with large joints and the hooves are well-shaped.

The most important feature of the Hanoverian, and one of the important tests that stallions have to undergo at Celle, is one of character: only horses with even temperaments and willing natures are allowed to breed. Hanoverians are noble and proud, with an excellent free-flowing action which allows them to excel at advanced dressage.

They come in all solid colours, often with white on the face and legs. Height is 15.2–17hh.

The Hanoverian's Thoroughbred breeding is clearly evident in its fine features and noble countenance.

HIGHLAND (U.K.)

Like all Scottish native breeds, the Highland has an ancient history, as the often-present, distinctive dorsal stripe indicates. The foundation breed is Celtic Pony mixed, over the centuries, with Galloway, which is now sadly extinct, plus various European breeds such as Percheron, Spanish, Barb and Clydesdale. In the 19th century, infusions of Arab blood were also added to bring the pony up to today's exacting standards.

The pony is not only native to the Highlands, but there is also a smaller variety which inhabits most of the Western Isles. It has always lived and worked with the Scottish crofters and was used in farming, forestry, haulage and general riding, where its equable temperament and sure-footedness were valuable assets. It was also taken to war, used in both the Boer Wars and the First World War.

Even though there has been a stud book for the Highland since the 1880s, there is no set breed standard;

consequently, there is quite a diversity of types and bloodlines. White marks, however, are frowned upon and stallions with anything other than small stars on their foreheads cannot be registered. The Highland has proved equally popular in other countries, and there are studs in Europe, Australia, the United States and Canada.

By the mid-1950s the Highland had achieved yet more popularity with the advent of pony trekking, where once again its temperament, sturdiness and agility made it suitable for both adults and children. In fact, the pony can carry up to 210lbs (95kg) with ease. Today the

Highland is used in a number of children's events, including jumping, cross-country, and pony club games, as well as in long-distance endurance events, showing and driving.

The Highland is a stocky, well-built pony. It has a small pretty head with a straight nose, small, often pricked ears, and large kind eyes. It has a strong body with a fairly long, well-developed neck, a neat shoulder, deep girth, and a well-muscled back. The legs are well-boned and sturdy, with hard, well-shaped hooves and feathering around the fetlocks. The mane and tail are thick and silky and are left untrimmed.

Highlands are friendly animals, with even temperaments and a willingness to work. They make excellent children's ponies, are hardy, require a little extra feeding, but will live out in all weathers. Their agility, intelligence and endurance makes them ideal for all pony events. They come in all solid colours, including grey and a variety of shades of fox, cream, gold, yellow and mouse. Height is up to 14.2hh.

The Highland is still useful for hauling logs in places inaccessible to vehicles. They are popular for showing – also for pony trekking and for driving.

HOLSTEIN (Germany)

The Holstein is probably descended from a native breed called the Marsh Horse, which once roamed the wetlands of the Elbe estuary in what is now called Schleswig-Holstein. The breed Holstein dates back to the 13th century, when Gerhard I, Count of Holstein and Storman, granted the monks of the monastery at Uetersen grazing rights for the quality horses which they bred. These were native stock mixed with Andalusian, Neapolitan and Oriental blood to produce a heavy, useful horse which was valued by farmers for its strength and reliability, and as a military horse for its courage, stamina, and ability.

By 1686 the Holstein was so respected that strict guidelines were introduced to protect and improve the breed, which had by now become popular throughout Europe. By the 18th century the Holstein's reputation was so great that vast numbers of horses were exported. Not all the horses were bred to exact standards, however, and the breed began to deteriorate.

By the 19th century the decline was halted, and measures were taken to save and improve the breed. As the demand for warhorses grew less, the Holstein was needed as a quality carriage horse; for this purpose, Yorkshire Coach Horses and Cleveland Bay stallions were mated with Holstein mares, which was a great success, and the breed received a new lease of life.

After the Second World War, Thoroughbred was also added to refine the breed, which also improved the Holstein's jumping ability and general character.

The Holstein is quite different from other warmbloods in that it has a large, rangy build with a huge stride. The head is long and straight with large, flaring nostrils. The ears are expressive and the eyes are large and gentle. The long neck is elegant and well-developed, with high withers; the back is long and straight. The shoulders are shapely and sloping, contributing to the huge stride. The chest is broad and the girth is deep, while the quarters are slightly sloping, muscular and powerful.

The Holstein is a beautiful, well-balanced horse with an amazing ground-covering, elastic stride. It is good-natured, obedient and eager to work. Its large size and scope means that it is much in demand as a top-flight competition horse.

They are most commonly bays, though all solid colours, together with greys, are permitted. These are large horses, standing between 16 and 17hh.

The Holstein is greatly respected as a competition horse, excelling as it does at dressage, showjumping and eventing.

HUÇAL (Poland)

Poland's Huçal, or Huzal, is a direct decendant of the now-extinct Tarpan, which once ran wild in eastern Europe. It is also related to the Konik, which shares similar breeding. The Huçal not only has native pony blood in its make-up, but it also has large amounts of Arab, received when it was deliberately bred for use in harness as well as for use as a general farm pony in the 19th century. This Arab blood, however, means that most of its primitive origins have become masked, but throwbacks appear from time to time which betray its Tarpan ancestry.

Because it originated in the Carpathian mountains of southern Poland, it is often referred to as the Carpathian. It is still bred today at a stud near Gorlice, where its role has changed very little. However, it does make a good children's pony.

The strong head, with its great character, indicates the Huçal's Oriental roots. The neck is of medium length and quite thick, but is carried well. The body is stout and sturdy with medium-length legs with good bone and very tough hooves.

The Huçal is bold, tough and courageous. It has a kind and willing disposition and its good balance and compact body make it ideal for work over mountainous terrain. It can survive in the harshest conditions and manages to exist on very little food.

The horses are mostly bay, with a dark stripe on the back, but they can also be dun, chestnut, black or dapple. Height is 12–13hh.

ICELANDIC (Iceland)

Iceland does not have its own indigenous breed of horse. The Icelandic is derived from the Fjord and Døle horses of Norway, and the Celtics, Shetlands, Highlands and Connemaras of the British Isles, which were brought to Iceland by Celts and Vikings in the 9th century. Because of the limited space on board their ships, the cargo would have consisted only of the best specimens and, once settled, the invaders would have allowed their horses to mate freely together to produce the Icelandic breed as we know it today. This resulted in a hardy animal which lived in a semi-wild condition and was able to survive Arctic

HORSES

winters. It was mainly used for farming and for riding over icy terrain.

It is interesting to note that in 982, the importation of horses was banned to prevent the spread of disease, as a result of which the Icelandic was allowed to interbreed; later selective breeding, however, means that conformation and health faults have been all but eradicated.

Historically, the Icelanders have been protective of their breed, wishing to preserve it in the country where it evolved. Nowadays, however, they are exported to other countries where they are popular as children's riding ponies as well as for trekking. Even though the Icelandic is a pony in stature, it is always referred to as a horse because there is no word for pony in the Icelandic language.

The Icelandic is well-constructed. The head is of medium length, having a typical pony character with small pricked ears and soft, expressive eyes. The neck is well-set, and the chest is broad with a deep girth. The body and legs are stocky and strong and the feet are extremely hard.

The Icelandic is ideal for children, being tough and hardy and happy to live out all year round. The pony has two extra gaits: the tölt, which is a running walk with four beats, and which is as fast as a canter and very comfortable; and the

flying pace, which makes great demands on horse and rider and which has two beats and is used for racing. The pony can reach speeds of up to 30mph (48km/h) and is impressive to watch. However, it is late to mature and should not be backed until the age of 4.

Icelandics live to a ripe old age, often working up until they are 30; in fact, an Icelandic in Britain is known to have died aged 42. Icelandics come in all solid colours as well as skewbald, palomino,

OPPOSITE & BELOW: The Icelandic evolved from ponies brought to the island by Celts and Vikings in the 9th century. Called horses, there is no word for pony in the Icelandic language.

dun and grey. One colour, silver dapple, is much prized, where the body is a rich brown and the mane and tail appear almost silver by contrast. In winter the coat is very thick with three distinct layers. They are usually 12–13.2hh, and very occasionally 14.2hh.

IRISH DRAFT (Ireland)

The history of the Irish Draft can be traced back to the Celts, who invaded Ireland and brought many breeds with them, most notably Oriental and Spanish horses which they mated with their Celtic Ponies. Later, in the Middle Ages, Ireland was settled by the Norman-English and their much larger, heavier horses would have been of European origin. These were bred with the Irish horse to produce a more substantial animal which was of use to farmers, being capable of ploughing, hauling, general riding, as well as hunting over Ireland's often difficult terrain.

By the 18th century the Irish Draft had been improved with additions of Thoroughbred and Arab blood and possibly also Barb and Turkmene. The result is a horse of excellent conformation, still capable of heavy work, but one which excels as a riding horse. It had all the docility and common sense of a heavier, coldblooded breed, but with the sparkle and verve of a hotblooded Arab or Thoroughbred.

During the Potato Famine of 1845–46 the Irish Draft's numbers diminished; Ireland's economy was in a state of turmoil and horse breeding ceased. But by the end of the century the breed had picked up, and there was a change of attitude when it was decided to introduce heavier stock, such as Clydesdale and Shire, to make it a much bigger, heavier draft horse. In 1917 a stud book was opened, but by the end of the First World War the breed was once again in danger, as mechanized transport began to dominate farming and haulage. By now, the Irish Draft was predominantly a riding horse, and a hunter in particular.

By the early 20th century, however, more Thoroughbred blood was introduced to produce the horse we know today. The breed is still predominantly a hunter, but it has been mixed with other breeds, particularly Thoroughbred, to make it a superb competition horse, which has inherited the Irish Draft's love of jumping, excelling at both cross-country and eventing. A little of the Irish Draft is also present in some steeplechasers.

HORSES

The head is neat, with the straight nose and medium-length ears producing a noble mien. The neck is shortish and very strong with slightly pronounced withers and a long sloping shoulder. The chest is broad and the girth is deep. The back is medium-length and well-muscled, with strong loins and sloping, powerful quarters. The legs are sturdy and muscular with good bone, and the hooves are large and round.

The Irish Draft has all the substance of a medium-weight draft horse, but its hotblood ancestry has also given it its refined appearance, there being no excess hair on the legs as in most heavier breeds. It has great stamina, agility and courage, and is generally good-natured and willing. Irish Drafts make excellent hunters: they will happily gallop over the roughest ground and jump almost anything in sight, while at the same time

OPPOSITE: The Irish Draft was bred as an all-rounder, as capable of work around the farm as it is of hunting all day over difficult terrain.

BELOW: Irish Drafts have Thoroughbred in their make-up, which is why they make such excellent showjumpers.

showing intelligence and common sense. Colours are usually bay, brown, chestnut and grey. Height is 15–17 hh.

ITALIAN HEAVY DRAFT (Italy)

The breed was first established in 1860 at the state stud at Ferrara by breeding native stock, i.e. Lombardy stallions from the Po delta with local mares. Arab, Hackney and Thoroughbred were also introduced to create a fairly lightweight horse which was used for light draft work.

By the 1900s, however, it was obvious that an animal with much greater strength and size was required, so existing mares were bred with Brabant, Boulonnais, Ardennais and Percheron. The result, however, was too large and cumbersome

The Italian Heavy Draft encompasses a variety of other breeds to make it a substantial though refined heavy horse.

and did not appeal to Italian sensibilities, so the lighter Postier Breton was added to produce a horse that was a heavyweight,

but not too large, and with plenty of agility and energy.

The head is rather small and fine for a heavy breed, with a broad forehead, straight nose, neat muzzle, and large nostrils. The ears are small and pricked and the eyes intelligent and alert. The neck is well-set, short, and very well-developed. The large shoulders and chest are muscular and broad with a deep, short body and large muscular hindquarters and loins. The legs are shortish and sturdy, with plenty of bone and a little feathering around the fetlocks.

Some Italian Heavy Drafts are lively and temperamental while others are quiet and docile. However, all are friendly and good-natured.

Usually chestnuts, some with flaxen manes and tails, but bays and red roans also appear. Height is 14.2–16hh.

JUTLAND HEAVY DRAFT

(Denmark)

The Jutland has an ancient and colourful history. It is descended from the coldblooded prehistoric Forest Horse, which much later mated with other indigenous stock to produce a heavy horse that was the favoured mount of armoured knights of the Middle Ages. The breed was further defined when Cleveland Bay and Yorkshire Coach Horse were added to give the horse more substance.

But it was the Suffolk Punch that really made the Jutland Heavy Draft the horse it is today. Selective breeding to improve the breed began in around 1850, the aim being to produce a strong horse suitable for the heavy draft work involved in farming. The breed was developed further in 1862 with the importation of a Suffolk Punch-Shire stallion cross called Oppenheim, which is the ancestor of the greatest Jutland stallion lines, in particular Aldrup Menkedal, which is now considered the foundation stallion of the breed.

The Jutland has also been influential in the formation of other breeds, such as the Schleswig Heavy Draft and the Danish Warmblood. The breed stud book was established in 1881.

The head is a little heavy and plain, with a slightly Roman nose. The ears are medium-length and the eyes have a soft,

kindly expression. The neck is set high, and is thick, arched and muscular. The withers are rather flat, merging into the broad back. The chest is broad, the girth deep, and the shoulders straight and muscular. The back is short with rounded loins and hindquarters. The legs are short, stocky and well-boned with plenty of feathering.

Jutlands have plenty of energy and a keen attitude to work, coupled with a kindly and calm temperament.

They often inherit the trademark chestnut of the Suffolk Punch, usually

The Jutland was orginally bred as a warhorse, but was refined by mating it with other breeds, most significantly the Suffolk Punch.

with a paler mane and tail, also coming in other solid colours as well as grey and roan. Height is 15–16hh.

KABARDIN (Russia)

The Kabardin is descended from the Tarpan – the wild horse of eastern Europe and western Asia, which sadly became extinct in captivity in 1887. The Kabardin remained unchanged in type until the Russian Revolution when, like many other Russian breeds, steps were taken to improve it. The original Kabardin was bred with Karabakh, Turkmene, Persian, and Arab to create a much bigger, stronger horse, which could be used for riding and general farm work, also as a pack animal.

This is an excellent mountain horse, being sure-footed, agile and intelligent, with the innate ability to search out the safest route. It has great stamina, enabling it to work all day under the harshest conditions without tiring.

BELOW & OPPOSITE: The Kabardin is descended from the now-extinct Tarpan. It was infused with other breeds to produce a large sturdy animal which is sure-footed and has great stamina.

The breed remains popular to this day in its place of origin, the republic of Kabardino-Balkaria, where it is still used for light draft work and for riding. Elsewhere, it is used as a competition horse and also to improve other breeds.

The head is quite long, often with a slightly Roman nose. The longish ears point inwards and are set close together. The eyes are wise and intelligent and the nostrils flared. The neck is long and well-developed and the back is straight and strong; the legs are long and fine but nevertheless very strong. The overall impression is of a horse with strong Oriental influences.

The Kabardin is a hardy breed capable of living out all year round, given extra feeding. It has a good constitution and mostly lives to a ripe old age. It is kind, obedient, trustworthy and intelligent. Colours are usually bay, black, brown and very occasionally grey. Height is 14.2–15.1hh.

KARACABEY (Turkey)

Turkey's horse population is very large and still plays an integral part in the day-

to-day lives of the Turkish people. They are used for general riding, farm work and haulage. Turkey has various types of horse, but the Karacabey is the only one to throw offspring which run consistently true to type.

It is known that the Karacabey is descended from native Turkish stock and is therefore considered to be the original Turkish horse. The breed itself is a relatively new one, beginning in the 1900s when native mares were bred with Nonius stallions which the Turks imported from Hungary; Arab was also added in large quantities to refine the breed and to add stamina, agility and speed. Today Karacabeys are still used for light draft work, riding, as a packhorses, and as mounts for the Turkish cavalry.

The head is proud with a straight nose. The ears are alert and of medium length, and the eyes are kind and intelligent. The neck is quite long and arched, the shoulders sloping, and the girth deep, with a medium-length body, good hindquarters and fine, strong legs.

The Karacabey is a sturdy horse with plenty of stamina and endurance. It is good-natured and a willing and obedient worker.

They come in all solid colours, also grey and occasionally roan. Height is 15.1–16.1hh.

KATHIAWARI (India)

Some are of the opinion that the original Kathiawaris were descended from horses brought to India by Alexander the Great, while another theory is that they sprang from the wild horses of Kathiawar. The breed that was in evidence over 100 years ago, however, was not a particularly attractive one, tending to be rather small and stunted as well as narrow in the body. It did, however, have assets which made it extremely useful: it was hardy, with

amazing stamina and endurance, and had the ability to work all day with very little sustenance. It also had tough, hard feet which enabled it to cope with the rough terrain.

This original stock was eventually enhanced by breeding it with Arab, which greatly improved conformation. The breed is mainly to be found in the province of Gujarat, which comprises Rajkot, Bhavnagar, Surendranagar, Junagadh and Amreli.

The Kathiawari's most striking characteristic is its ears, which point inward, almost meeting in the middle. The ears are also extremely mobile and can rotate 180 degrees. The head is fairly long, with a slight Roman nose, the forehead is broad, and the eyes are large, kind and intelligent. Much of the horse's Arab inheritance is immediately obvious, it being lightweight with fine legs, but with a predisposition to sickle hocks.

Very hardy and strong, the horses are most commonly chestnut, but other varieties are possible, including bay, grey, dun, and coloured.

Their height is 14–15hh, depending on regional differences.

The Kathiawari is thought to have originated from stock brought to India by Alexander the Great. By far its most distinctive feature is its curly ears.

KLADRUBER (Austria)

The breed was established in 1597 by the Emperor Maximilian II of Austria, where it was bred at the Kladruber Stud which is situated in the former Czechoslovakia. Today the stud still produces Kladruber horses, which are composed of many different breeds. Heavy Alpine mares were originally mated with Barb and Turkish stallions, then later with Andalusian, Neapolitan and Lipizzaner, resulting in horses that were used exclusively to draw coaches and appear in the parades of the Austrian Court in Vienna.

The Second World War, however, eventually took its toll of the breed with numbers plummeting to dangerously low levels; it was therefore decided to revive and improve the breed by adding Anglo-Norman, Hanoverian and Oldenburg blood, which were infused into the remaining stock. Today, the Kladruber is doing well and is used for general riding and for light haulage.

The Kladruber has inherited many of the attributes of the Andalusian, Neapolitan and Lipizzaner. The head is noble with a broad forehead, straight or slightly Roman nose, medium, well-shaped ears, and an alert expression with

The Kladruber is impressive and proud. It is an amalgam of many breeds, including Andalusian, Neapolitan and Lipizzaner, to name but a few.

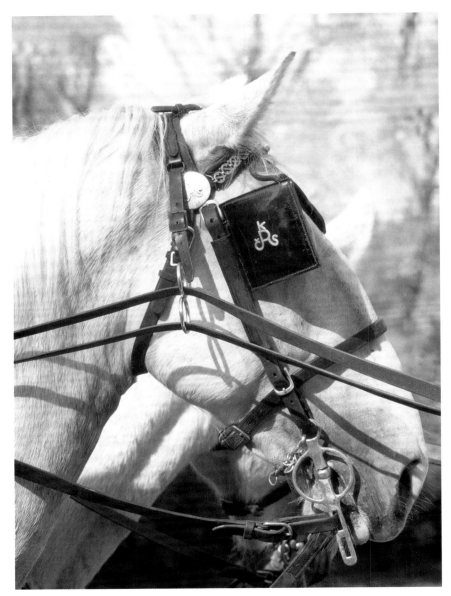

160

large, kind and intelligent eyes. The neck is high-set and well-developed; the girth is deep, and the chest broad. The body is of medium length and is sturdy with large quarters. The legs are well-muscled with good bone and well-shaped hooves.

The Kladruber has an equable temperament and is a willing and obedient worker. It has an attractive high-stepping action. Colour is usually grey, though blacks are also bred. Height is 16.2–17hh.

KNABSTRUP (Denmark)

The Knabstrup's origins go back 200 years or so, but its ancestry is far more ancient, dating back to the prehistoric Forest Horse. The Knabstrup is unusual for a European horse in that it has a distinctive spotted coat. This is thought to be inherited from prehistoric forebears, many of which were spotted, as can be seen in ancient cave paintings.

In the 16th and 17th centuries spotted horses were very popular at European courts, but the Knabstrup was founded much later, in the early 1800s, when an Iberian mare of the Knabstrup Estate in Denmark was mated with a palomino Frederiksborg stallion. The foal was born with a spotted coat of many colours, which also had an attractive sheen. This became the foundation stallion of the Knabstrup breed.

Unfortunately, because subsequent horses were bred primarily for their unusual coats, insufficient care and attention was given to their conformation, leading to gradual deterioration, when the breed lost its popularity and almost disappeared. In recent years the horse has

The Knabstrup's most distinctive feature is its spotted coat, which makes it popular as a circus performer. However, it is predominantly a general riding horse.

been improved with the addition of Thoroughbred blood and is popular once again. Today it is used as a general riding horse and also features in showing classes and, because of its spots, even the circus.

Their head is large with a straight or Roman nose. The ears are small and well-pricked and the eyes have a kind, gentle expression. The muzzle is square with large, open nostrils. The neck is high-set and there are well-developed shoulders and a broad chest. The back is rather long, with slightly sloping quarters, and the legs are strong with good bone. The mane and tail are rather sparse.

The Knabstrup is a good-quality riding horse with excellent natural paces. It is kind and intelligent, easy to train, and an obedient and willing worker. Height is 15.2–16hh.

There are various colour permutations similar to the Appaloosa, such as white with chestnut, bay and black. One overall colour or roan is also possible.

Blanket White over the quarters and loins with a contrasting base colour.

Spots White or dark spots over all or on a portion of the body.

Blanket with Spots A combination of the above.

Roan Blanket Partially roan, with patterning usually over quarters and loins.

Roan Blanket with Spots A roan blanket which has spots within it.

Leopard White with dark spots.

Snowflake There is dominant spotting over the quarters and loins.

Frost White specks with a dark background.

KONIK (Poland)

The Konik, or 'little horse', resembles the wild Tarpan of eastern Europe and western Asia which is now extinct. The Konik itself is not a specific breed and there is no particular standard. However, there are around five types, some with native blood and others with Arab added.

The Konik, being related to the Tarpan, which was a small horse of Oriental origin, has a small, neat head, dorsal stripe, and zebra markings. Sadly the last remaining Tarpan died in captivity in 1887, having been hunted to extinction some ten years earlier.

In the last century efforts were made to revive the ancient breed by preserving the Konik's Tarpan genes. These reconstituted Tarpans, as they are now known, live wild in a nature reserve where they are beginning to manifest many Tarpan characteristics. Today Koniks are mainly used for farm work and occasionally as children's ponies.

The Konik's strong head with great character shows its Oriental origins. The neck is of medium length and quite thick, but with a good carriage. The body is stout and sturdy with medium-length

The Konik is the closest relative to the now-extinct Tarpan and attempts are being made to preserve the Tarpan gene pool present in the breed.

legs with good bone, which are slightly feathered, and tough hooves.

The Konik is hardy and will live out all year round with little extra feeding and care. Some can occasionally be wilful and difficult – a throwback to their wild Tarpan origins.

Usually light-brown or dun, bays sometimes appear. The mane and tail are full and the dorsal stripe and zebra markings are sometimes visible. Height is 12.2–13.2hh.

LATVIAN (Latvia)

The Latvian is thought to have an ancient history, though no one can be certain of its origins; but the general opinion is that it is either descended from the prehistoric Forest Horse, a heavy type that once roamed over northern Europe, or that it evolved from an indigenous pony crossed with Tarpan and Arab blood. It is thought that the latter is more likely.

Today there are three distinctive types of Latvian, depending on the other breeds with which it has become intermingled. The heaviest is the Latvian

Draft, which is the original breed present in the other two and which has been infused with Finnish Draft, Oldenburg and Ardennes to make a substantial draft horse which is not so heavy that it cannot be ridden. The medium-sized version is the Latvian Harness Horse, which came into being in the 1920s when the original Latvian was bred with Hanoverian, Oldenburg and Norfolk Roadster to make a lighter and more elegant carriage horse. The final, lighter, Latvian is a more recent addition, having received infusions of Arab and Thoroughbred to

Latvians come is three distinctive types, the ones that are lightest in weight being used as competition horses.

make a horse which is rather more of a warmblood, and does well in competition. Today all three are still used by farmers and competition riders.

The three types may vary in stature, but they are all unmistakeably Latvians. The head is longish and noble with a straight nose and large nostrils, proud eyes, and small well-shaped ears. The neck is long and nicely placed, with sloping shoulders, a deep girth and a longish body with well-developed quarters. The legs are shapely though volume of bone depends on type. The mane and tail are thick and full.

Latvians are incredibly strong, and they are endowed with excellent stamina and equable temperaments.

All solid colours and the occasional grey are possible. Height is 15.1–16hh.

LIPIZZANER (Austria)

The Lipizzaner is probably one of the world's most recognizable breeds, due to its association with the Spanish Riding School of Vienna. Despite its origins in what is now Slovenia, the Lipizzaner has a much more ancient history, dating back to the 8th century and the Moorish occupation of Spain. The Moors brought

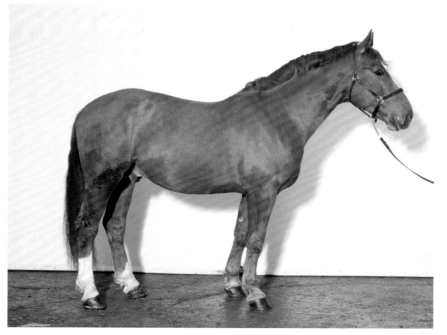

with them horses of Oriental origin, such as Arabs and Barbs. These were bred with the heavier Iberian horses, which in turn produced the Andalusian which is the most important element in the Lipizzaner's breeding.

In 1580 Archduke Charles, son of the Holy Roman Emperor Ferdinand I, and who had inherited Austria-Hungary, sought to improve his horses, deciding to school them in *haute école*, a form of equitation that featured spectacular leaps into the air, which was becoming increasingly popular. To this end he founded a stud at Lipizza, which also specialized in breeding carriage horses, and filled it with quality Spanish (Iberian) horses, known to be capable of the discipline. He used these as the foundation stock of the Lipizzaner, crossing them with heavier native breeds as well as Barb, Arab, Andalusian and other European breeds such as Neapolitan and Kladruber. Thus, over a period of several hundred years, the classic riding horse was born.

The Spanish Riding School of Vienna, that most famous riding establishment, had been founded in 1572. The name was not due to its Spanish

A Lipizzaner stallion on display at the Spanish Riding School of Vienna. The name was adopted due to the Spanish origins of the famous horses.

riding traditions but because of the Spanish origins of the horses. The aim of the school was to teach the art of classical equestrianism to men of noble breeding. The original venue was a crude wooden structure, which was replaced by the splendid building which was comissioned by Charles VI in 1735 and which is still in use today. The Spanish Riding School is stocked exclusively with Lipizzaner stallions.

When the Austrian-Hungarian Empire collapsed, the stud was moved to Piber in Austria, and during the Second World War was evacuated to Germany for its own protection. Today, the Lipizzaner is bred mainly at Piber (which supplies all the stallions for the Spanish Riding School) but also at Lipizza and Babolna in Hungary, and in the Czech Republic, Slovenia and Romania. Nowadays, as well as performing in the Spanish Riding

BELOW LEFT: Only Lipizzaner stallions are used for *haute école* in the Spanish Riding School.

OPPOSITE: Lippizaner mares and their foals at the Piber Stud in Austria.

School of Vienna, the Lipizzaner is also used as a draft horse and for carriage driving. They are also becoming popular as general riding horses.

The Lipizzaner breed was based on six foundation stallions, and their different characteristics can be seen in its descendants today. Lipizzaners can therefore vary according to which of the six bloodlines has been used, but generally speaking they are of an Iberian type, similar to the Lusitano and Andalusian. The head is large with either a straight or Roman nose. The ears are finely pointed and alert and the eyes kind and intelligent. The neck is well-set, powerful and well-muscled with a good crest. The chest is wide with a deep girth. The shoulders can be slightly straight and short. The back is long but strong and muscular with powerful quarters and a slightly low-set tail. The legs are shortish but powerful, with small, well-shaped, tough hooves.

The noble Lipizzaner possesses all the qualities of its breeding: the agility and balance of its Iberian forebears as well as the stamina and refinement of the

Oriental. It combines stamina and endurance with natural balance and agility, is kind, intelligent, willing and obedient, but with plenty of sparkle. It is late to mature, usually around the age of 7, and should not be worked too young.

However, it stays sound for a long time and usually lives to a good age.

The Lipizzaner is famous for its grey (white) coat. Foals are born dark, but most lighten to become pure white as they mature. Very few remain brown or black.

Traditionally, the dark Lipizzaners are kept at the Spanish Riding School as reminders of their Spanish forebears, which were bay, black, brown or roan. This is quite a small horse, growing no larger than 15.3hh.

LUNDY (U.K.)

The Lundy is not a true native breed, but was created in 1928 by crossing New Forest mares with Thoroughbred, Welsh and Connemara stallions. The resulting ponies were then turned loose on Lundy Island in the Bristol Channel, where they bred further to produce semi-native ponies. The breeding programme was not as successful as anticipated, but a few ponies still remain on the island.

This is an attractive pony that is full of character. The head is fairly large with a full mane, a straight nose, neat muzzle, and large kindly eyes. The ears are small and alert, the body is long, and the legs are sturdy with slight feathering.

The Lundy is hardy enough to live out all year round, even in harsh winter conditions, and requires little extra feeding, confirming that it is a breed with plenty of stamina. It is also sure-footed

The Lundy is full of character and practically looks after itself, even in the harshest of conditions.

and agile. The Lundy is kind and willing, and makes a good children's pony if caught and broken in while still young.

The ponies come in all solid colours as well as grey and dun. Height is around 13.2hh.

LUSITANO (Portugal)

The Lusitano shares a heritage with the Andalusian, both having descended from the Iberian riding horse. The Lusitano gets its name, which was only adopted in the early 20th century, from Lusitania, the Roman name for Portugal. The origins of the breed go back to around 25,000 BC to the ancient ancestors of the Sorraia breed, which can be seen in cave paintings on the Iberian peninsula.

Unlike the Andalusian, the Lusitano's breeding has remained much truer to its Sorraia ancestry, with infusions limited to Oriental, Garrano and Spanish blood. This mix hasn't changed for centuries and today care is taken only to use horses with obvious Iberian characteristics to keep the breed true to type.

The Lusitano was bred mainly for working the farms around the fertile River Tagus, where it is still used – also in bullfighting, known as the *corrida*, as well as in *haute école*. In Portugal the bull is thankfully not killed, and the whole event is performed with the rider on horseback. The Lusitano, therefore, has to be incredibly agile and fast to avoid injury.

These horses are highly prized and receive *haute école* schooling to enhance their precision so that they can survive the demanding and dangerous spectacle. The Lusitano stallions are trained to these

high standards before they are sent to stud, and all fighting horses are left entire, because it is thought that geldings lack the courage and intelligence to work in such a dangerous environment.

Today they are still used in bullfighting – also in the lower levels of dressage. Infusions of Lusitano are also used to improve other breeds.

The Lusitano has a noble countenance. The head is quite long, with a straight or slightly Roman nose and flared nostrils. The ears are of medium length, well-shaped and alert. The eyes

are keen and intelligent, the neck is set high with a well-developed muscular crest and well-defined withers. The sloping shoulders are powerful and the chest is broad with a deep girth. The back is short and strong and the loins broad, with quarters that are not too large. The Lusitano's high-stepping action is attributed to its strong, long hocks, which are capable of great impulsion, with deep flexion achieved by a well-developed second thigh (stifle).

This noble and courageous horse is kind, good-natured and obedient. It is level-headed and not given to panic, important attributes in a fighting horse.

All solid colours are acceptable as well as grey. Height is 15–16hh.

The Lusitano has a shared heritage with the Andalusian of Spain, both being descended from Iberian stock, though the Lusitano has remained slightly truer to its origins.

MALOPOLSKI (Poland)

The Malopolski, also known as the Polish Arab, was bred originally to be a general riding and driving horse, which could also be utilized on farms. It is based on native Mazuren and Posnan stock, although the two breeds now barely exist, having been incorporated not only into the Malopolski but also into its distant relative, the Wielkopolski (page 251). The breed also has a good deal of Arab in its make-up, as suggested above – also Thoroughbred, as well as Gidrán and Furioso from Hungary.

The Malopolski is now split into two, depending on which of the two Hungarian breeds is dominant. The Darbowski-Tarnowski has a predominance of Gidrán blood and Sadecki Furioso, with the result that there is no definite conformity. Today the breed is used mainly as a competition and riding horse, but is still also used in harness.

The Malopolski's head is very Arab in appearance, being wedge-shaped with a slightly dished or straight nose, depending on the strain. The ears are small and shapely and the eyes lively and intelligent. The neck is high-set, long, and elegant, with a slight crest; the shoulders are sloping, with a broad chest and a deep girth. The hindquarters are well-muscled with a high-set 'Arab' tail. The legs are long with plenty of bone, ending in well-shaped hooves.

The Malopolski is an excellent jumper, making it a good all-round performance horse. It has a lively and spirited temperament that requires skilful handling.

All solid colours as well as grey and roan are permitted. Height is 15–16.2hh.

The Malopolski is a well-bred, spirited horse which excels in competition.

MANGALARGA MARCHADOR (Brazil)

For centuries Brazil and Portugal were closely connected and at one time were under the same ruler, Don Joao VI, in around 1815. It was he who brought quality Portuguese and Spanish horses to Brazil, particularly the Altér Real and Andalusian.

The Mangalarga is a direct descendant of one particular Altér Real stallion which was mated with Criollo mares; later, more Altér Real, Barb and Andalusian was added to improve the breed, the result being a neat, lightly-built horse that is strongly reminiscent of the

Barb, but with the rolling gait of the Spanish breeds.

It is most often used for riding the enormous estancias of Brazil, where its fifth gait, known as the *marcha*, makes it fast but comfortable for the rider. The *marcha* is a cross between a trot and a canter, which the horse is able to maintain for great distances. The horse's name is a combination of the words Mangalarga, from the name of the *hacienda*, and *marcha*. Today the Mangalarga Marchador is also used for endurance and trail riding, jumping and polo. It is therefore an excellent all-round riding and showing horse.

The head is high and proud with medium-length ears and intelligent eyes. The nose is straight with flared nostrils. The back is long with strong loins and neat quarters; the shoulders are sloping with a deep girth, and there are well-muscled legs with hard hooves.

The Mangalarga has incredible stamina which enables it to work all day and cover huge distances. It is good-natured, willing and obedient.

Bay, grey, chestnut and roan are the usual colours. Height is around 15hh.

The Mangalarga Marchador is neat and lightly built. It also has a fifth gait – the *marcha*.

175

MAREMMANA (Italy)

The foundation of the Maremmana originally rested on the now-extinct Neapolitan, with later infusions of Andalusian and other European stock. The breed became virtually extinct, however, having been weakened over the centuries by matings with local semi-wild horses from the Tuscan region of Maremma, as well as with any other horses or ponies that appeared in the vicinity. More recently, Thoroughbred has been added, which has greatly improved the horse's quality, although its hardiness has suffered as a result. Today, the Maremmana is still used on farms and as a general riding horse, and is also used by the Italian mounted police.

The head is rather plain and workmanlike, with a straight or slight Roman nose. The neck is short with a straight shoulder, flat withers, and a low-set tail. The legs, however, are strong and sturdy with good, tough hooves.

The Maremmana has been blessed with a calm temperament. It is reliable, obedient and willing to work. All solid colours are permitted, including grey and roan. Height is 15–15.3hh.

The Maremmana is used by the Italian mounted police – also in farming.

MARWARI (India)

The Marwari, from the Marwar region of Rajasthan, is similar in appearance to the Kathiawari (page 158), but is of much greater stature, and has featured in Indian art over the centuries. The Marwari is unusual in that it has a fifth gait, called the *revaal*, which is a long, smooth action with little vertical movement and very comfortable for the rider. Marwari numbers declined during the British occupancy of India, but thanks to today's

Rajput families and others interested in the continuation of the breed, the Marwari is once again flourishing. It is now used as a dancing horse, popular at weddings and festivals. The dance is a form of *haute école*, which the horse would have been taught when it was a warhorse long ago.

The Marwari has a high, proud head-carriage with a straight or Roman nose, its trademark ears curving inward until they almost join together in the centre. The eyes are large, bright and intelligent; the neck is of medium length and arched in movement. The coat is fine and silky.

The Marwari has a naturally flamboyant presence and the will to perform. However, it is also tough and is able to survive harsh conditions. It is courageous, intelligent and a willing worker.

The horses come in all colours, including roan, piebald and skewbald. Height is 15–16hh.

The Marwari was once a great warhorse and featured in Indian art for centuries. Thanks to renewed interest, the breed is once again gaining in popularity.

MECKLENBURG (Germany)

The Mecklenburg State Stud at Redefin was founded in 1812, but the breeding of the Mecklenburg horse actually dates back earlier to the start of the 18th century, when horses were bred there to supply the Duke of Mecklenburg-Schwerin's stables, and which were destined to improve the quality of horses throughout the country.

The older type of Mecklenburg was a heavy, cob-like animal suitable for the cavalry; but it was the infusion of Thoroughbred which made it famous throughout Europe. Throughout the 19th century the Mecklenburg was further refined with more Thoroughbred; unfortunately, some inferior stock was used and the breed deteriorated in quality, making the offspring more difficult to

Today's Mecklenburg has been strongly influenced by the Hanoverian. Its accurate paces makes it a good dressage horse.

sell. The breeders attempted to rectify the problem by introducing heavier horses back into the bloodline, but this did nearly as much damage. Eventually, a happy medium was found and the breed was stabilized.

Today the Mecklenburg has been further developed, making it a horse suitable for leisure and competition riding. It has been heavily crossed with the Hanoverian.

This is a workmanlike horse, with sturdy limbs and a kind face. It is suitable for most equestrian disciplines.

The Mecklenburg has a bold yet tractable temperament, making it ideally suited to both ridden and carriage work.

Coat colour may be bay, brown, black or chestnut. Height is 15.3–16.1hh.

MÉRENS (France)

Ponies remarkably similar to the Mérens, and depicted in ancient cave paintings at Niaux, have roamed the Pyrenees of Andorra since prehistoric times. The native breed has changed slightly over the years, having received infusions from heavy horses arriving with the Romans – also Oriental bloodlines.

The Mérens has been used for ploughing and hauling for hundreds of years by mountain farmers, where its

TThe Mérens is kind and level-headed, making it a good children's pony. It also works well in harness.

stamina and sure-footedness make it suitable for the inhospitable terrain. The Mérens was also used for transporting lumber, by soldiers in the Middle Ages, and by Napoleon during his campaigns.

The Mérens, or Ariègeois, is similar to the British Dales and Fell ponies and the Friesian, and breeders still raise their stock in the traditional way. The ponies live out all year round, the foals being born during the spring snows. In the summer, transhumance occurs when they are herded up high into the mountains. Here, they are allowed their freedom for several months, after which time some are selected for breaking, selling on, or breeding. Today they are still used for farming and forestry and also as children's ponies.

The Mérens is a most attractive pony, with a small, neat head, a slightly dished or straight nose, small pricked ears, and kind, soft eyes. The neck is short and well-developed, and the body strong and stocky with well-developed hindquarters. The legs are shortish with good bone and a little feathering around the fetlocks.

The Mérens is well-balanced, level-headed and compliant –also energetic. It is tough and is able to withstand the harshest of conditions.

The horses are usually black, with thick manes and tails. Height is 13–14.2hh.

MISSOURI FOX TROTTER
(U.S.A.)

The Missouri Fox Trotter was developed in the 19th century by settlers in Missouri and Arkansas. Initially, its purpose was to be a general riding horse with the speed and endurance to cope with difficult terrain. The foundation stock for the breed was the Morgan, which was infused with Thoroughbred and Arab as well as with Iberian bloodlines. As horses with elaborate gaits became more popular, the breed was later mated with Saddlebred and Tennessee Walking Horse, which greatly improved its elegance, bearing and paces, including its foxtrot gait; this is basically a diagonal gait like the trot, in which the horse appears to walk with the front legs while trotting with the hind.

In the early days, before racing was made illegal, the Fox Trotter had been a useful competitor, but after the ban it was once again used as a general riding horse.

A stud book for the breed was eventually opened in 1948. The breed society, however, placed strict guidelines that the Missouri Fox Trotter should have

Unlike the Saddlebred, the breed standard for the Fox Trotter bans any artificial aids to improve its natural paces. The foxtrot pace is a cross between a walk and a trot and is very comfortable for the rider.

no artificial aids to influence and enhance its gait, such as nicking or setting the tail; consequently its action is not as pronounced or extravagant as, for example, that of the American Saddlebred. The breed is popular in the United States, where it is used for general riding, showing and endurance.

Their head is a little plain, with a straight nose and a square muzzle with large open nostrils. The ears are medium-length and the eyes have a kind but intelligent expression. The neck is medium-length with prominent withers; the back is short, with strong loins and hindquarters. The tail is set fairly low; the

legs are long with large joints and well-shaped, strong hooves.

The Fox Trotter has a charming, easy-going temperament. It is willing and obedient with plenty of stamina and endurance.

All colours as well as part-coloureds are acceptable. Height is 14–16hh.

MORGAN (U.S.A.)

One of America's most famous and versatile breeds, all Morgans can be traced to a single stallion by the name of Figure. It was later renamed Justin Morgan, after its owner, Thomas Justin Morgan, a tavern-keeper and singing teacher, who had decided to supplement his income by breeding stallions.

The colt was born in around 1790 in Vermont. It is thought that its sire was called True Briton, and was probably a Welsh Cob, but little is known concerning the dam; it is believed, however, that she had some Oriental and Thoroughbred blood in her make-up.

Thomas Justin Morgan was so impressed with Figure's looks and personality that he eventually decided to put him to stud. The results were remarkable, in that offspring the image of their father were always produced, no matter what mare had been used in the mating. The performance of each foal,

The elegant Morgan is a truly remarkable breed in that it stemmed from only one particular stallion. Whatever the mare covered by this stallion, the foal always minutely resembled its sire, both in appearance and ability.

moreover, was second to none, its sire's prowess as a marvellous harness and riding horse having been replicated in the offspring, making it difficult to believe that such a significant and impressive breed should have developed from just one stallion.

Today Morgans are just as versatile – used in harness competitions, shows, driving, trail riding and driving.

The horses are strong, versatile and hard-working,with a spirited but tractable nature.

The head should give immediate evidence of quality, with beautiful and expressive eyes. The muzzle is small and the profile straight or slightly dished. The neck is well-crested and the shoulders strong. The hindquarters are large and strong and the legs sturdy.

Some Morgans are bred particularly for their high-stepping action, a type known as the Park Morgan. The other type is the Pleasure Morgan, whose action is less exaggerated.

All solid coat colours are acceptable. Height is 14–15.2hh.

MURAKOSI (Hungary)

The Murakosi or Murakoz is a relatively recent breed, created in the 1900s to be used in general agriculture and as a draft horse. It was founded on Hungarian native stock, crossed with Brabant, Percheron, Noriker and Ardennais heavy horses. Today, through selective breeding, two distinctive types have emerged – one heavy and one light. Today the breed can still be seen working on farms in its native Hungary.

For heavy breeds, both types have good conformation. The head is well-proportioned and large, reminiscent of the Ardennais, with a straight or slightly

Roman nose, medium, well-shaped ears, and a kind, honest look. The neck is muscular with a slight crest and the shoulders are strong; the chest is broad with a deep girth. The body is shortish and well-balanced, with short, clean legs, plenty of bone, and a little feathering.

The horses are physically very strong, with good temperaments and positive attitudes to work.

It is most often chestnut, with a flaxen mane and tail – less often black, brown, bay or grey. Height is around 16hh.

The Murakosi is a well-balanced draft horse with a kind and positive attitude to work. It is still used on farms in Hungary.

MURGESE (Italy)

The Murgese comes from Apulia, the region of south-east Italy that extends into the 'heel' of the peninsula and which is known as Puglia in Italian. The original breed is probably about 500 years old, being descended from native Italian breeds intermingled with Barb and later Thoroughbred.

In the 15th and 16th centuries the breed was used by the Italian cavalry. Over the centuries, however, the Murgese virtually died out, only to be revived in the 1920s; a stud book was opened in 1926. Today the Murgese in a rather inferior light draft horse which has no specific conformity.

The head is rather plain but with a kind honest expression. The general appearance is similar to that of the Irish Draft, although the hindquarters tend to be weak with a low-set tail.

The Murgese has some jumping ability and is used as a general riding horse. It has a kind nature and is a willing worker.

Usually chestnut, grey or black coats are also possible. Height is 14–15hh.

Murgese are often ridden by Italian mounted police. They are similar in stature but not as fine as the Irish Draft.

MUSTANG (U.S.A.)

Although horses were once present in North America, the original prehistoric horses had long been extinct by the time the conquistadors arrived in the 16th century. The Spanish brought Iberian horses with them in their ships, derived mainly from Arabs and Barbs, and many of these sleek, desert-bred, resilient horses were allowed to wander off, spreading into North America and forming feral herds in their new environment.

Native American tribes came to value the Mustang's qualities and many were caught and domesticated by them. They even developed their own breeds based on the Mustang, such as the Appaloosa, the Cayuse Indian Pony, and the Chickasaw Indian Pony, also known as the Florida Cracker Horse.

By the beginning of the 19th century there were between one- and two-million Mustangs in existence, many of which ran free, but others were domesticated and used by settlers. Unfortunately, the wild horses came to be regarded as pests and were culled by the thousands to make room for cattle. But it wasn't only the ranchers who were responsible for the decimation of the population. Thousands were killed in the 20th century, sacrificed to the pet-food industry.

HORSES

Sadly, there are fewer than 50,000 Mustangs in existence today and in some areas numbers are dangerously low. Determined efforts are now being made to safeguard the breed for the future and, fortunately for the Mustang, the breed is now considered an important part of the American heritage and a protected species.

Mustangs come in all colours, sizes and builds, although horses which display Barb characteristics are most favoured by breeders.

Easy to train, due to their intelligence, Mustangs are tough and

The Mustang developed from horses that arrived with the Spanish conquistadors, many of which were turned loose in their new country to form the basis of the breed as it is today.

resilient. Colours are usually brown, chestnut, bay and dun. Height 14–16hh.

NEW FOREST (U.K.)

It is likely that the New Forest pony is a descendant of the Celtic Pony, as are all the British native breeds, though the earliest mention of it dates to the time of King Canute (c.995–1035), who famously sought to stop the sea's rising tide.

The New Forest is located in the county of Hampshire in southern England and consists mainly of scrubland, bog and moorland, which has led to the development of a hardy animal designed to survive harsh conditions. Over the years, Thoroughbred and Arab blood have been introduced, mainly to increase size and performance and to improve the pony's appearance, but is was not until the end of the 19th century, during the reign of Queen Victoria, that a structured breeding programme was initiated. At the same time, other British breeds were also introduced, such as the Dartmoor, Exmoor, Welsh, Fell, Dales and Highland.

RIGHT: New Forest ponies are plentiful and can easily be seen when driving through the New Forest in Hampshire.

OPPOSITE: New Forest ponies are excellent all-rounders for children and teenagers. They are kind, willing, and good at jumping.

In 1891, the Society for the Improvement of New Forest Ponies was founded to ensure that there was an ample supply of quality stallions living in the New Forest, and this in turn led to the official publication of the first stud book in 1910. Nowadays, although still living and breeding in their home environment, many quality New Forest ponies are also bred in private studs all over the world.

This is one of the larger breeds native to Britain. It is an ideal child or teenager's pony and is also excellent for driving. It has a well-proportioned body that is more slender than other British breeds, together with well-formed feet.

New Forests have lovely temperaments. They are calm, good-natured and a pleasure to own. They are substantial enough for dressage, showjumping, cross-country; in fact, it is often said that a good New Forest pony can rise to any occasion.

Any solid colour is acceptable. Height is 12–14.2hh.

NONIUS (Hungary)

The Nonius was developed by the famous Mezőhegyes Stud of Hungary which acquired a young stallion when it was captured by the Hungarian cavalry from a French stud in 1813, following Napoleon's defeat at Leipzig. The horse, called Nonius Senior, was of mixed Anglo-Norman and Norfolk Roadster parentage. It wasn't particularly attractive and many conformation defects were present, such as weak quarters and a short neck. Moreover, its plainness was not enhanced by big ears and small eyes. Nonius did have an excellent temperament, however, being willing, obedient and easy to handle, and the Hungarians must have thought him promising because they began a programme to produce the excellent Nonius breed.

They experimented by putting Nonius Senior to many different mares, such as Arabs, Kladrubers, Normans, Lipizzaners and English cross-breeds. They then selected the best of his daughters to mate with him, with the result that certain traits began gradually to emerge, and which set the breed standard. Nonius Senior died at the age of 22 after an extremely productive career and his sons and daughters continued the line with further refinements of Arab and Thoroughbred blood added.

There are two kinds of Nonius: a heavy type suitable for carriage driving

LEFT: There are two types of Nonius: a heavier one used as a driving horse and a lighter riding horse.

OPPOSITE: The Nonius, though rather plain, has many excellent qualities, such as amiability and a willingness to work.

as well as farm work, and a lighter version, mainly used as a cavalry or riding horse. Today, both make good all-rounders.

Nonius Senior's conformation defects have largely been eradicated. The head is rather long, with medium-length ears, large kind eyes, and a straight or Roman nose. The neck is of medium length and well-developed. The chest is fairly broad, with a deep girth and sloping shoulder. The back is long and straight with good quarters and long legs.

The Nonius is prized for its willing, equable temperament.

They are usually black, dark brown or bay with only a little white on the lower legs and face. The large Nonius is 15.3–16.2hh, the smaller one being 14.2–15.3hh.

NORIKER (Austria)

The Noriker is also know as the South German Coldblood, the Pinzgauer, and the Oberlander. The breed is an ancient one dating back to the time of the Roman Empire, when several heavy breeds, possibly with Andalusian and Neapolitan blood flowing in their veins, were introduced to the province which now equates with modern Austria, but which was then known as Noricum.

The breed which developed from these heavy horses was strong and sure-footed, making it ideal for draft work in difficult mountain conditions where it was used for farming and forestry. By the 16th century the breed had been given an infusion of new blood in the form of Andalusian and Neapolitan, which brought a degree of finesse and agility to the breed. By the 19th century a South German strain had developed and this was improved by the addition of Norman, Cleveland Bay, Holstein, Hungarian, Clydesdale and Oldenburg, which made the breed much lighter and more elegant.

As well as the heavy breeds in its bloodline, the Noriker was later refined with additions of Andalusian and Neapolitan, which made it rather more agile than most draft breeds.

Today there are five different types of Noriker, all of which are lightish draft horses still used for farming in Austria and Germany.

The head is medium-sized and rather plain, with a straight or slightly Roman nose. The Noriker has a placid look. The neck is short, well-developed and strong, with a straight shoulder.

The body is sturdy with sloping quarters and a low-set tail. The legs are short with good bone, hard hooves, and a little feathering.

For a draft horse, the Noriker's breeding has made it quite active and agile. It is strong and its sure-footedness makes it suitable for difficult terrain. It is amenable and obedient and copes well with harsh conditions.

Norikers are most commonly chestnut, often with flaxen manes and tails, also bay, brown, black, roan and spotted. Height is 15.1–16.2hh.

NORMAN COB (France)

Coming from Normandy in north-western France, as the name suggests, this is a region famous for breeding good-quality horses for many hundreds, even thousands of years. The breed was established in the 17th century as an all-round workhorse, suitable for riding, carriage, and farm work. Its breeding includes Anglo-Norman, which was a useful base for riding, and lightweight harness horses, together with Norfolk Roadster and the native stock of the area.

Typical of the cob type, with a large head and body and short legs, the main difference is that the Norman is a much larger animal than the average cob, which stands around 15hh.

In France, Norman Cobs are usually docked, a practice illegal in many countries, particularly the United Kingdom. The breed is popular elsewhere, and French studs are willing to lend their stallions out to private breeders. They are still used for light draft work and are also very comfortable to ride.

Although the body is stocky, the Norman Cob has a refined appearance, with a high, proud, head-carriage, medium-length ears, a straight or slightly Roman nose, and bright, intelligent eyes. The neck is of medium length and well-developed, while the body is strong with a broad chest and stocky legs.

The Norman Cob is a quality horse with an active gait. It has great stamina and a charming personality.

They are usually chestnut, bay and brown; very occasionally grey or roan. Height is 15.3–16.3hh.

Although quite stocky, the Norman Cob still manages to look rather refined. It is much larger than most cobs, usually over 15.3hh, which makes it a useful draft as well as riding horse.

NORTH SWEDISH (Sweden)

This is another breed that can trace is origins back to the prehistoric Celtic Pony. It shares much of its ancestry with the Norwegian Døle, and has Friesian, Norfolk Trotter, Heavy Draft and Thoroughbred in its make-up.

The breed has split into two distinctive types: the lighter version known as the North Swedish Trotter, which is capable of covering 0.62 mile (1km) in 1 minute 30 seconds, and which is faster than many other breeds recognized for speed. The heavier draft type is of greater stature and is used for general farm and haulage work.

Like the Døle, the breed resembles a large pony. The head is small and neat with a broad forehead, straight or slightly Roman nose, and a squarish muzzle. The ears are small and alert and the eyes kind and inquisitive. The neck is short and well-developed with a slight crest. The chest and shoulders are powerful, the girth is deep, and the back is long with well-muscled hindquarters. The legs are rather short but sturdy, with good bone, hard hooves, and feathering around the

The North Swedish looks rather like an overgrown pony, and like most ponies requires little care or extra feeding. It is full of character and has plenty of stamina.

heels. The heavy type has rather more bone and substance.

The North Swedish is tough, hardy and can expect to live a long life. It requires little care and feeding and has great stamina and endurance. It has a well-balanced, springy action; the trotting type has a good turn of speed.

Coats may be in all solid colours. Height is 15–15.2hh.

OLDENBURG (Germany)

This is the heaviest of the modern German warmbloods, originally bred as a coach horse. It dates back to the early part of the 17th century, when keen horse-breeder Count Anton Guenther of Oldenburg, in north-western Germany, began the first breeding programme.

The Oldenburg's earliest ancestors were heavy Friesian horses infused with Spanish and Arabian blood. The breed was stabilized in the 19th century by the introduction of Thoroughbred, Cleveland Bay, Yorkshire Coach Horse, Anglo-Norman, and Hanoverian stallions.

Though originally bred as a coach horse, the Oldenburg was also used by the military as a strong artillery horse.

Oldenburg Olympic Bonfire, a famous competitor ridden by Anky Van Grunsven.

As the years passed, however, the need for such horses diminished and a demand for lighter riding horses for competition and pleasure arose. In the second half of the 20th century lighter breeds were again introduced, such as Thoroughbred, Trakehner, Hanoverian and Westphalian. Nowadays, the Oldenburg excels at dressage and showjumping while retaining its ability as a carriage horse, still used for the purpose today.

The Oldenburg is distinguished by a noble head and a proud,

workmanlike air. It has a high-set neck, long shoulder, strong back, and a well-muscled croup with strong joints. With its large frame and long, active stride, it makes a elegant dressage horse or a powerful showjumper.

The Oldenburg could be said to resemble a hunter type. Its character is equable, making it a pleasant horse to handle and own.

Coats may be black, bay, or brown. This is a large horse with a height of 16.2–17.2hh.

TThe Oldenburg has a varied pedigree based on Friesian, Spanish and Arabian blood, which was later refined with Thoroughbred, Cleveland Bay, Yorkshire Coach Horse, Anglo-Norman and Hanoverian.

ORLOV TROTTER (Russia)

The Orlov, or Orloff, Trotter is one of the foremost breeds of its type in the world. It was founded in the 18th century by Count Alexey Orlov, whose ambition was to produce a superb trotting horse, and to this end founded a stud at Ostrov, near Moscow. He brought in a large number of Arabians, among them two distinctive stallions – the beautiful, silvery-grey Smetanka, and the brown Sultan I. After one season, Orlov was left with a few progeny from Dutch Harddraver, Mecklenburg, Danish, Thoroughbred and Arabian mares.

Orlov was not happy with his stud and wanted somewhere better with more grazing, which he found in Khrenovoye in the Voronezh region to the south of Moscow, a place he considered perfect for his purpose, with vast areas of grassland, clear, natural springs, and a dry climate.

The Khrenovoye Stud was thus founded in 1778, and the following year produced a colt called Polkan I, which in turn was mated with a Danish mare carrying Spanish blood. The result was a foal called Bars I, which eventually showed exceptional stamina and trotting abilities and became the foundation stallion of the Orlov breed.

The Orlov is a muscular horse, famous for its exceptional and impressive action. Its stamina and quality ensured that it reigned supreme on the racetrack until the end of the 19th century, when Standardbreds and later French Trotters were introduced to the Russian racing scene. Unfortunately, the Orlov is now in crisis, due largely to the introduction of these faster breeds.

The Orlov has a small, elegant head with a noble profile. The ears are highly reminiscent of the Arab's. Hindquarters are powerful and, like many trotters, the shoulders are straight.

The horse is nergetic, sure-footed and bold. Owing to its swift, balanced trot it is suitable for riding and driving as well as trotting.

Coat colour is usually grey, black or bay. Height is 15.2–17hh.

The Orlov Trotter is famous above all for its impressive action. It is a well-bred attractive horse and was once the toast of the 19th-century racing fraternity. Today, however, because faster breeds have overtaken it, such as the French Trotter and Standardbred, the Orlov is in imminent danger of decline.

PASO FINO (Puerto Rico)

The foundation of the Paso Fino is old Spanish or Iberian stock, having inherited the same bloodlines as the horses brought to the Americas by the Spanish conquistadors in the 16th century; however, different environments have caused slight variations in their evolution in terms of character and conformation.

The Paso Fino is a naturally gaited horse, like the Peruvian Paso or Stepping Horse (page 206) and another lesser known breed from Colombia, and although it is predominantly a working horse on the coffee plantations of Puerto Rico, these gaits make it particularly remarkable. They are spectacular to watch, the main ones being the *fino*, the classic gait of the show ring, performed with the horse balanced and collected; the *corto*, executed with only medium collection and light contact on the bit; and the *largo*, the speed form of the gait.

There are another two variants, the *sobre paso*, this being a much more natural gait in which the horse is allowed a loose rein and is relaxed, and which is used in general riding rather than the show ring; the other is the *andadura*, which is a fast pacing gait. This is uncomfortable, however, and is only performed for short periods. The

rest of the time the horse's effortless movements make it extremely comfortable and smooth to ride, its gliding action making it popular for trail riding. Paso Finos are also in great demand for showing and for displays.

The head is fine, almost Arab-like, with a straight nose and flared nostrils, longish well-shaped ears, and intelligent eyes. The body is very Spanish, similar to the Andalusian's, with a good

The Paso Fino is famously known for its spectacular gaits – the *fino*, *corto* and *largo* – which are smooth, effortless and comfortable for the rider.

sloping shoulder, well-developed neck, and medium-length back with slightly sloping quarters and a low-set tail. The legs are sturdy and strong with large hocks.

The Paso Fino has an excellent temperament. It has great enthusiasm and is obedient and easy to ride, seemingly enjoying the company of human beings. Despite its small stature it is very strong; in fact, even the smallest will easily carry a man over hills and rough terrain.

All colours are acceptable. Height is 14–15hh.

PENEIA (Greece)

The Peneia is a breed native to the Greek mainland, likely to have been infuenced by Oriental breeds, particularly Arab. For centuries it was used as a packhorse, for light draft work, and also for riding, where its strength, agility and sure-footedness were great assets. Peneia stallions are also bred with female donkeys to produce hinnies.

The head is of medium size and rather plain, with a straight nose, smallish intelligent eyes, and alert ears. The body is small, wiry and underdeveloped. The legs are of

The Peneia is a sure-footed, wiry little workhorse.

medium length, fine though strong, with tough, hard hooves.

The Peneia is kind and willing. It is strong with plenty of stamina and endurance. The coat may be any colour. Height is between 10.1 and 14hh.

PERCHERON (France)

The Percheron comes from La Perche in Normandy in northern France. The breed is an ancient one dating back to 732, when Arab horses, abandoned by the Saracens after their defeat at the Battle of Poitiers, were allowed to breed with the local heavy mares of the region. From these matings the Percheron type emerged.

At this time the horse was much lighter than its modern counterpart and was used for riding as well as for light draft work. The type remained popular until the Middle Ages and the Crusades, when Arab and Barb horses from the Holy Land were mated with the Percheron. It was also around this time that the Comte de Perche brought back Spanish horses from his forays in Spain; these were also mated with the Percheron, with further infusions of Andalusian added later. By the 18th century, the original breed had become

almost completely eradicated by the addition of Thoroughbred and more Arab; in 1820 two grey Arab stallions were mated with Percheron mares, which is responsible for the predominantly grey colour of the modern-day breed.

By now all the heaviness of the ancient breed had disappeared; consequently, heavy mares from other regions were bred with Percheron stallions to make them more suitable for agriculture and to formulate the breed as it is known today. The lighter Percheron still exists and is used as a heavy riding horse, while the heavier version is still used for farm and forestry work and, in some countries, for pulling drays. It is also popular in the show ring.

Over the years the Percheron has been heavily exported to other countries, such as the United Kingdom, Canada, Australia and other parts of Europe, which has helped its recognition as one of the world's leading heavy breeds.

For a heavy breed, the Percheron's head is proud and elegant, with a straight nose, broad forehead, expressive eyes, and short shapely ears. The neck is short to medium, well-developed and with great strength. The shoulders are nicely sloping and well-shaped, with a broad chest and a deep girth. It is fairly short in the back, which adds to its strength, with slightly sloping but broad quarters. The legs are short and sturdy with well-shaped, tough hooves with very little feather.

The Percheron possesses a good deal of elegance due to the large amounts of Arab blood which have been added over the centuries. It has an excellent temperament, is calm, obedient and easy to handle, and has a keen intelligence. It has a smooth but lively action, making it very comfortable to ride.

Coats are mainly grey but are There are two types of Percheron: the light version is used as a riding horse, while its heavier counterpart is still used on farms and for forestry work.

occasionally black or dark chestnut. Percherons come in two sizes, small (14.1–16.1hh) and large (16.1–17.3hh).

PERUVIAN PASO (Peru)

The Peruvian Paso, or Peruvian Stepping Horse, shares much of its descent with the Paso Fino, the national horse of Puerto Rico, the foundation of both breeds being Barb and old Spanish or Iberian stock brought to the Americas by the conquistadors in the 16th century.

The Peruvian Paso has adapted well to its environment and has the ability to carry riders great distances over dangerous mountain terrain in safety and comfort. It has also adapted to the high altitude of the Andes and has a larger, stronger heart and greater lung capacity than other breeds, which enables it to function energetically in areas where oxygen is scarce.

Like the other Paso breeds, the Peruvian has the natural ability to perform the attractive four-beat lateral gaits that make riding long distances so comfortable for the rider without tiring the horse. There are three gaits: the *paso corto*, used for practical purposes; the *paso fino*, an exaggerated slow gait used in the show ring and in parades, which has the appearance almost of

Like the Paso Fino, the Peruvian Paso has the *fino*, *corto* and *largo* gaits which are passed from mare to foal and which are therefore entirely natural.

slow motion; and the *paso largo*, which is fast. These traits are passed from mare to foal and are completely natural, needing no artificial aids to accomplish them. Once a person becomes accustomed to the gaits

(the horse never trots or gallops) the Peruvian Paso makes an excellent riding horse.

In stature, the Peruvian Paso is similar to its cousin the Paso Fino. The head is fine and resembles that of the

Barb, with shapely pricked ears and a proud, alert look. The nostrils are readily dilated, presumably to allow as much oxygen as possible to be taken in. The body has all the evidence of a Spanish inheritance and is similar to the Andalusian's. The legs are sturdy, quite long, and well-muscled with hard hooves.

This horse is hardy and energetic but also equable and intelligent. It is an obedient and willing worker.

They may be any colour, but bay or chestnut is usual, with white permitted on the head and legs. The mane and tail are abundant, with fine, lustrous hair that may be straight or curly. Height is 14–15.2hh.

HORSE BREEDS

PINTO (U.S.A.)

The Pinto or Paint Horse (from the Spanish *pintado*, meaning 'painted'), like many of the old American breeds, is descended from Iberian horses that came over from Spain with the conquistadors. They are also sometimes called 'Calico' horses in America.

In England and other anglophone countries they are referred to as 'piebalds' (black and white) or 'skewbalds' (any other colour and white) because their coats, of any solid colour, are heavily mottled with white; alternatively they are merely referred to as coloured horses, although in the United States the Pinto is regarded as a separate breed.

The original Spanish horses were allowed to revert to a feral condition

The Pinto or Paint Horse came about when Iberian horses brought over by the conquistadors were allowed to run wild. The striking patterned coat makes the Pinto a most arresting and dramatic sight.

and gradually extended into North America, where they roamed the Western deserts. Once domesticated

by Native Americans, however, they were greatly revered; in fact, the Pinto was even believed to possess magic powers.

Ranchers also adopted these hardy horses, as their stamina and agility made them excellent for work over extensive distances. Today they are still used as workhorses but also at rodeos, and for trail riding and showing and as all-round riding horses.

The Pinto has a fine head and graceful well-defined neck. The ears are alert and of medium length, while the eyes indicate spirit and intelligence. They are usually quite short in the back, with long, strong legs and hard tough hooves. They are hardy and agile. Height is 14.2–15.2hh.

The Pinto is well-known for its striking coat, which can be black, chestnut, brown, bay, dun, sorrel, palomino, grey or roan, patched with large areas of white. There are three distinctive types of coat pattern: **Tobiano**, in which the head is like that of any solid-coloured horse, but there are round or oval spots resembling shields running over the neck and chest. One or both flanks may be coloured white or a colour can predominate. The tail is often composed of two colours.

Overo, which is predominantly dark or white, though the white shouldn't cross the back between withers and tail. The head should be white with scattered irregular markings on the rest of the body. At least one leg should be dark and the tail is usually one colour. **Tovero**, which is a mixture of the two.

POITEVIN (France)

Also known as the Mulassier, and possibly not quite as attractive as the other heavy horses, the Poitevin comes from a low-lying area of west-central France and is the least known of the French breeds; for this reason it is the most endangered.

For centuries it was used for little else than the breeding of very strong mules out of Poitevin mares, the breed having originally been created using Flemish horses which were brought to Poitou in the 17th century to drain the marshes; they also contain Shire and Clydesdale bloodlines.

At one time the Poitevin had a rather primitive appearance, but selective breeding has done much to improve the breed. It is lighter than most draft horses, and has a lively, springy gait.

With the advent of motorized transport the mule trade was greatly diminished and with it the Poitevin; it was only saved by the dedication of a few breeders who had been working with Poitevins for a long time and had become attached to the breed. It remains extremely rare, with only around 400 remaining.

The Poitevin has a medium-sized head with a straight nose, small ears, and a kindly expression. The neck is shortish and well-developed, with strong shoulders, a deep girth, and a broad chest. The body is shortish with a straight back and large, rounded quarters. The legs are of medium length and sturdy, with plenty of bone and feathering. The mane and tail are left long.

The Poitevin is an exceedingly rare breed, with approximately 400 remaining examples.

Placid and calm with a quiet intelligence, Poitevans have a rather active gait.

The may be various shades of grey, dun and black. Height is 15–16hh.

These ponies are most popular with children (though strong enough to carry a small adult), as they are kind, obedient and easy to handle. They also do well in competition.

The breed had the appearance of a small horse rather than a pony, and at a later date was further refined with Quarter Horse and Arab blood to produce the showy, high-stepping action popular in the show ring today.

Similar in stature to British Thoroughbred ponies, the Pony of the Americas is most popular with children, who find it easy to handle. It is also strong enough to carry a small adult and is used in endurance, trail riding and showjumping as well as in trotting and pony flat racing.

The head is very Arab, with a broad forehead, small pricked ears, and a straight or slightly dished nose. The eyes are large and kind. The body is of medium length with a good sloping shoulder, well-developed quarters, and fine but strong legs.

The Pony of the Americas is strong and hardy with a calm but willing disposition.

Colour ranges are similar to those of the Appaloosa. Height is 11.2–14hh.

PONY OF THE AMERICAS
(U.S.A.)

This is a relatively new breed dating to the 1950s, and is the result of an accidental cross between a Scottish Shetland Pony and an Appaloosa mare with Iberian origins. The resulting offspring, Black Hand I, turned out to be a smaller version of its dam and it was this stallion that became the foundation of America's first pony breed.

POTTOK (France and Spain)

The Pottok, or Pottock (which means 'a prehistoric animal hunted by cavemen'), is an ancient native breed with mysterious origins, but it has always inhabited the west of the Basque region as well as Navarra, in Spain, and south-west France, where it remained a pure breed until the 8th century when it was bred with Arabs. Pottoks have been used on farms and as pit ponies in the coal mines of northern France.

The Basques have a great affection for the pony and it remains an important part of their culture. Many still live in a semi-wild state and some are used as general riding ponies. They are excellent jumpers, and are also used for trekking, where their sure-foodedness and familiarity with the terrain are great assets.

The head is small and neat with a straight or slightly Roman nose. In winter, the Pottok grows a moustache to protect the nose when foraging for food among cold, sparse vegetation. The neck is short and strong with a thick shaggy mane; the chest is broad,

The Pottok is from the Basque region of France and is held in great esteem by the local population. It still lives in a semi-wild condition.

and the loins are long with slightly sloping hindquarters. The tail is low-set and very thick. The legs are strong with well-shaped, hard hooves.

Pottoks have lively temperaments and are willing workers. They are also good-natured, strong and hardy, and have excellent powers of endurance. They come in all solid and part-colours. Height is 12–13hh.

PRZEWALSKI'S HORSE (Mongolia)

This is a truly ancient breed, also known as the Mongolian or Asiatic Wild Horse, which is stocky and dun-coloured with a dark-brown erect mane. Primitive horses of this kind were hunted by man 20,000 years ago, and the likenesses of similar horses can be seen in prehistoric cave paintings in

HORSES

Spain and France. Now almost certainly extinct in the wild, as no sightings of it have been made for over 30 years, it is the only true wild equine and the ancestor of the domestic horse.

The earliest written evidence of its existence was in the 9th century and later in 1226, when a herd of wild horses are supposed to have caused Ghengis Khan, founder of the Mongol Empire, to fall from his horse.

Because of its isolation and the fierceness with which stallions protect their mares, the Mongolian horse's bloodline remained pure and can be traced back to its primitive ancestors. It gets its modern name from the man who brought it to the attention of the

world, Colonel N.M. Przewalski, a Polish explorer, who acquired the remains of a wild horse in 1881 from hunters who had discovered them in the Gobi Desert of western Mongolia. He took them to the zoological museum in St. Petersburg, where naturalist I.S. Poliakoff examined them and decided they belonged to a species of primitive wild horse. Following the discovery, some of the living horses were captured and kept in captivity in zoos and wildlife parks in order to save them from total extinction.

The captive population has increased rapidly and is carefully monitored at Prague Zoo, which holds the stud book of the breed. The horses

are kept in as natural conditions as possible and some have been released back into the wild in China, Russia and Mongolia, where they are a protected species; there is also a successful population in France.

The head is of medium size with a broad forehead and a straight or slightly dished nose. The eyes are set high on the head and are rather small with a wild look. The nose tapers to a narrow muzzle with small, low-set nostrils. The body is strong, with a longish, straight back, a thick, short neck, and weak quarters. The legs are short and stocky with hard, tough hooves.

Przewalskis are never tamed and can be aggressive and ferocious, especially in the presence of their young. They need little care as they are extremely hardy.

They may be various shades of dun, ranging from yellow to red. They have black manes and tails and black legs, often with zebra markings. There is a black dorsal stripe running down the back. The muzzle and around the eyes are creamy white. Height is 12–14hh.

Przewalski's Horse is almost certainly extinct in the wild, but a few survive in captivity. The breed has all the characteristics of horses seen in prehistoric cave paintings.

QUARTER HORSE (U.S.A.)

The first breed to become established in the United States was the Quarter Horse; consequently it holds pride of place in the hearts of all American horse-lovers.

The Quarter Horse's origins can be traced back 500 years to the time when the Spanish conquistadors brought Iberian and Oriental horses to Florida.

English colonists eventually acquired these horses from Chickasaw Indians, which they crossed with their own English horses, mainly Thoroughbreds, then refined them again with more Thoroughbred blood.

The name Quarter Horse comes from the horse's ability to sprint for short distances over a quarter of a mile (0.4km); before the days of racetracks,

the early colonists would race their horses down main streets, which were usually about this distance in length. The powerful hindquarters of the Quarter Horse gave it great acceleration and even today it is faster than the Thoroughbred over short sprints.

Not only was the Quarter Horse good at racing, it also made a good riding horse, pulled wagons, and made

an efficient packhorse. However, its most valuable attribute was its natural instinct to round up herds. This was undoubtedly a legacy from its Iberian forebears which already had plenty of cow-sense, having worked the bullrings of Portugal and Spain, and which had nerves of steel and amazing agility. Today, however, racing predominates, but their use in rodeos, trailing, and as all-round family mounts is widespread across the United States, Canada, Australia, and even parts of Europe.

Quarter Horses can be quite large due to the influence of the Thoroughbred. The head is relatively small and the eyes are bright and set far apart. The neck, hindquarters and back are extremely muscular, which makes the feet appear small in contrast. The tail is set quite low.

The Quarter Horse is easy to maintain, enthusiastic, honest and energetic. All solid colours are acceptable. Height ranges between 14.2 and 16hh.

The Quarter Horse has been strongly influenced by the Thoroughbred, which is apparent from its fine appearance. It is truly excellent at herding and cutting cattle, a skill illustrated here at a rodeo.

SALERNO (Italy)

The Salerno was developed in the Campania region of Italy, based on the sadly now-extinct Neapolitan – a superb horse of Iberian, Andalusian and Arab descent. It was most attractive and was so highly prized that a breeding programme was established to make further improvements. It is probably the best and most handsome of today's Italian saddlehorses.

By the late 19th century there was deep unrest in Italy and the Salerno's breeding programme was abandoned. However, a few managed to survive and by the 1900s breeding was re-established when the existing horses were crossed with Arabs and Thoroughbreds. The result were used by the cavalry and as elegant carriage horses.

The breed continued to develop and more English Thoroughbred was added to produce a superb horse of the highest quality; this had excellent paces, jumping ability, speed, stamina and grace.

The quality head is fine with a broad forehead, straight nose, and flared nostrils. The ears are medium-length, shapely, and expressive. The eyes are indicative of intelligence and spirit. The neck is long and beautifully arched, with sloping shoulders and a good broad chest. The girth is deep and the back straight, with strong loins and well-developed hindquarters. The legs are fine but strong and muscular, with good hard hooves.

The Salerno requires an experienced rider, in that it has a spirited and lively temperament. It does, however, respond well to training, when it is usually obedient and acquiescent.

Salernos come in all solid colours and stand around 16hh.

The Salerno is a highly-prized Italian saddlehorse. It has excellent paces combined with speed, stamina and elegance.

SELLE FRANÇAIS (France)

Many of the best-known breeds are a fusion of several others and the Selle Français is no exception. Breeders of this fine warmblood had been working for many years in their quest for the ultimate competition horse, and accordingly used a variety of breeds to achieve their goal. Finally, in the 1950s, the breed was given official status and was named the Selle Français or French Saddle Horse.

Its main ancestor is the Norman, dating back to the Middle Ages, itself a cross between indigenous mares and imported horses such as Arabs and other Orientals. The Norman's primary use was as a warhorse, but the line had also been influenced by German and Danish carthorses, along with Thoroughbred and Norfolk Roadster. Other infusions, such as Limousin, Charentais and Vendéen, have also played their part in the production of the modern Selle Français.

However, it was mainly Thoroughbred which was responsible for the athletic horse we know today. The breed excels as a competition horse and is particularly talented at showjumping, though it is a good eventer and hunter.

The Selle Français is an elegant horse. The standard demands a fine head, sloping shoulders, and well-sprung ribs. The legs should be strong and the hindquarters powerful. There are up to five weights to suit individual tastes.

Like many of the warmblood breeds, the Selle Français has an even, placid temperament, but is also intelligent, willing, and energetic enough for top competition.

They are mainly chestnut, although other colours are acceptable. Height ranges between 15 and 17hh.

The Selle Français is a combination of many breeds, from the heavy Norman to the English Thoroughbred, which was used to improve the breed and to produce a top-flight competition horse.

SHAGYA ARABIAN (Hungary)

The Shagya Arabian comes from Hungary's second most famous breeding establishment, the Babolna Stud, founded in the late 1700s; the other one is Mezöhegyes. In 1816 the military stipulated that all brood mares should be bred with Oriental stallions to provide cavalry and harness horses; stallions with mixed Oriental blood as well as Iberian crosses were also used. The results, although fairly lightweight, were horses that were tough and with plenty of stamina.

Following this success it was decided that the Bobolna Stud should concentrate on breeding horses with predominantly Arab blood, which was the beginning of the excellent Shagya Arabian.

Today's breed is descended from one Arab stallion, called Shagya, which was brought from Syria in 1836. He was fairly large for an Arab, standing at 15.2½hh, and was from the Siglavi or Seglawy strain. The stallion was typically Arab in conformation, with a fine dished nose, a proud high-crested neck, short body, and high-set tail. It was mated with the military-style mares to produce the first Shagya Arabians and subsequent breeding by selection has produced a beautiful, refined riding horse of the highest quality. Today Shagya Arabians make excellent riding and competition horses and are also used for driving. They remain popular in their native country but are relatively rare elsewhere.

The Shagya is very like the Arab in conformation, but is a little heavier. The head is wedge-shaped with a wide forehead and a straight or dished nose. The ears are neatly pointed and alert

and the eyes kind. The muzzle is small and delicate with large flaring nostrils. The neck is finely arched, well-muscled, and set high. The shoulders are sloping, with a broad chest and a deep girth; the body is fairly short, with well-defined quarters and long, elegant legs which are well-muscled at the top with more bone than that of the traditional Arab.

The Shagya has the constitution of the Arab but is bigger and stronger. It is kind, noble and spirited, with great stamina, speed and agility.

Coats come in all solid colours, though many inherit the grey of the Shagya stallion. Rarest of all is black. Height is 14.2–15.2hh.

Shagya Arabs stem from one stallion, Shagya, which was imported to Hungary from Syria in 1836.

SHETLAND (U.K.)

The Shetland islands lie off the coast in the far north of Scotland. The islands are remote and have a harsh climate, particularly in winter. There is not much shelter for the ponies and food is scarce, but they have adapted admirably to survive on very little and next to nothing during the winter months, when they are known to come down from the hills and feed on seaweed that has been washed up on the beaches.

It is unclear where the ponies originally came from, but there is evidence that they have been on the islands for a very long time, since Bronze Age remains were found dating from 2,500 years ago. Alternatively, they may have come from Scandinavia across the ice, or even from Europe.

Traditionally, Shetlands were used by islanders as riding, ploughing, pack and harness ponies. In 1870, the Londonderry Stud at Bressay, Scotland, fixed the type and character of the breed and, although no longer in existence, all of today's best stock can be traced back to the famous Londonderry sires.

The head is small and neat and can be slightly dished. The ears are small and the eyes open and bold. The neck, shoulders and withers are well-defined; the chest and quarters must be strong and muscular. The mane and tail is profuse, with straight feathering on the legs. The coat is double-layered, a feature unique to the Shetland.

The Shetland has plenty of character and can be wilful at times. Because it is relatively strong for its size, it may be too much for a small child, unless it has been properly trained and has good manners. However, when kept in a suitable environment, with adult help on hand, they make superb children's ponies.

Of unclear origin, Shetland ponies are thought to have been living on Shetland for at least 2,500 years. Today they make good children's mounts and often appear in driving and showing classes.

Coats can be black, brown, bay, chestnut, grey, piebald and skewbald. Their height is up to a maximum of 42in (107cm).

SHIRE (U.K.)

The Shire is one of the most famous and distinctive of all the draft horses and one of the largest and most majestic breeds in the world. Descended from medieval warhorses, whose immense strength enabled them to carry knights wearing full armour into battle, the Shire was probably based on the Friesian, with later infusions of Brabant. It was brought to England by the Dutch to drain the fens of East Anglia, but it was not until the late 19th century that the best heavy examples in England were selected to develop the breed as it is known today.

The Shire's strength also made it suitable for agriculture and heavy haulage work, so initially the breed was established in Lincolnshire and Cambridgeshire, where strong horses were required to cope with the heavy fenland soil. Eventually, however, the Shire became widespread in Staffordshire, Leicestershire and Derbyshire until it ultimately became widespread over the whole of England.

Up until the 1930s, the Shire was widely seen across the country, but the numbers dropped dramatically as farms began to make use of tractors until the breed was in danger of disappearing altogether. Fortunately, the problem was realized by a few dedicated breeders who helped to promote the breed and restore its popularity.

The Shire Horse Society has worked tirelessly to raise funds and to encourage the spread of the breed to other countries. Today there are active Shire Horse societies across Europe, the United States, Canada, and Australia. Although a few Shires are still used on farms today, it is mainly for the sheer pleasure of working them in their traditional roles. They are also used in ploughing competitions, again, for pleasure, and for the same reason breweries use them in pairs to deliver beer locally, using normal mechanized transport for longer distances; the spectacle of these beautiful horses is obviously excellent publicity.

The Shire's most significant feature is its sheer size and massive muscular conformation. It is the largest and strongest horse in the world and when mature weighs a ton or more. Built ultimately for strength, the chest is wide, the back short-coupled, the loins

and quarters massive. The legs, joints and feet are sufficiently large to balance and support the Shire's size; the lower legs are covered with long, straight, silky feathers; iIn the show ring, white feathers are generally preferred as they help to accentuate the horse's action. Even though the Shire is such a large horse, it is not an ungainly heavyweight; in fact it is very much in proportion and quite beautiful to behold. The head is always noble and the nose slightly Roman. The eyes are large and wise.

The Shire is well-known for its patient, gentle and placid nature; it is a true 'gentle giant'. In fact, it is quite amazing that such a strong animal, that weighs so much, can be so easily handled, and it is not uncommon to see them ridden or handled by children or small women. Their kindness is legendary.

Shires may bay, black, brown or grey, which are the recognized colours of the breed. White feathers on the legs are preferred for the show ring and white face-markings are common. Height is between 16.2 and 18hh.

Shires stem from medieval warhorses, strong enough to carry knights and their heavy armour into battle.

SORRAIA (Portugal)

The Sorraia was discovered in Iberia by
a Portuguese zoologist, Ruy d'Andrade,
in 1920, when he was fascinated to
learn that a wild horse subspecies was
alive and well in Europe. Many
disputed that it was a truly wild horse,
however, and some thought it
impossible that one could have survived
in a pure state, with no contact with the
horses that man had already had a
hand in breeding.

When Andrade researched further
into the genetics of the Sorraia he
found that it had a similar skull and
teeth to those of the Andalusian and

Lusitano. He therefore concluded that
the Sorraia was the wild ancestor of
both these breeds.

The Sorraia is a light-coloured
pony with a dorsal stripe along the
back and zebra stripes on the legs. Due
to its rarity, inbreeding has been
intense; however, this has not affected
its hardiness. At first glance the Sorraia
looks a little like a Lusitano.

Like many of the world's wild
horses, the Sorraia is independent and
hardy. It is able to survive on the most
meagre pasture and even without the
provision of shelter in winter. It is a
good packhorse

Coats are dun or grey. Height is
12.2–13.2hh.

The Sorraia is an ancient breed with the dorsal
stripe and zebra markings of its prehistoric
ancestors. The Sorraia itself is a forebear of the
Andalusian and Lusitano.

STANDARDBRED (U.S.A.)

The Standardbred is famous for its trotting and pacing abilities and is widely used in harness racing throughout the world. The breed dates back 200 years when trotting races became sufficiently popular to warrant a breeding programme for the purpose.

The founding sire of today's Standardbred was Messenger, a grey Thoroughbred, born in 1780 and imported to Philadelphia in 1788. While Messenger had been bred for traditional racing at a gallop, his own sire, Mambrino, had been responsible for a long dynasty of famous trotting coachhorses in England.

Messenger worked at stud for about 20 years and became famous for producing strong, talented trotters. Meanwhile, during the mid-1800s in New England, the Morgan breed was being used to produce a line of smaller trotters with a straight, up-and-down action. The high-stepping action of the Morgan line was then combined with the long-reaching stride of the Messenger line, which increased the performance of the Standardbred to a great degree.

This Standardbred is in action on the Red Mile Track at Lexington, Kentucky.

HORSE BREEDS

The trot of a Standardbred appears huge in comparison with that of ordinary breeds and is a gait whereby the legs are moved in diagonal pairs. However, the 'pace' is peculiar to this breed and is a gait where the horse moves its legs in lateral pairs. While the trot is natural to all horses, the pace generally has to be taught, although some Standardbreds will offer to pace from birth. Pacing is quicker than trotting as it allows the stride to be longer and therefore more economical.

The term Standardbred was introduced in 1879 and derives from the time standard which was set to test the ability of harness racers. The Standardbred horse is required to cover a mile (0.6km) in 2 minutes and 30 seconds. Since this first standard was set, improved breeding has enabled the modern Standardbred to beat this target easily.

The head is in proportion with the horse's body and the eyes are kind; the ears are indicative of alertness. The horse is muscular overall, with a well-sprung barrel, sloping shoulder, and a strong back. The legs resemble those of the Thoroughbred, though are somewhat larger, with large joints; the hooves are large and strong.

The Standardbred has an excellent temperament, and away from the racetrack is quite placid. When racing, however, it is highly competitive, and displays great stamina and almost unbounding energy.

Coats may be all solid colours, but bay, black, brown and chestnut are the most usual. Height is 14.2–17.2hh.

The Standardbred is probably the most successful trotter, having been used in trotting races all over the world for the past 200 years.

SUFFOLK PUNCH (U.K.)

The Suffolk Punch originated in East Anglia in England and takes its name from the county of Suffolk, 'Punch' being an old word for short and thickset. It is thought to date back to 1506 and it is the oldest heavy breed in Britain.

First developed by crossing the native heavy mares of the region with imported French Norman stallions, modern-day Suffolks, however, can be traced back on the male side to a single, nameless stallion, foaled in 1768, and which belonged to Thomas Crisp of Orford, near Woodbridge, Suffolk; even though the breed was relatively pure, infusions of Norfolk Trotter, Thoroughbred and cob were added during the following centuries.

BELOW & PAGE 230: The Suffolk Punch is Britain's oldest breed, dating back to 1506. Sadly, it is rare today.

The Suffolk Punch is immensely strong, but due to its relatively small size it is also quite agile. These qualities, combined with a lack of feather on the legs, like the Percheron, made it ideal for working

the heavy clay soils of East Anglia. Moreover, food consumption, in proportion to its size, is also small, which enabled it to work long days on farms without stopping.

As with many of the heavy breeds, numbers fell dangerously low when farm tractors became widespread. Today Suffolks are rare, even though there has been a concerted effort in recent years to increase numbers. Today, Suffolks are shown, used in ploughing competitions, or are owned by breweries.

The Suffolk Punch is always chestnut in colour (the traditional spelling for this particular breed is chesnut, without the 't'). The breed is well-known for its great strength and has an extremely powerful, muscular body with relatively short legs providing a low centre of gravity, which in turn helps the horse to pull ploughs or vehicles more easily. Suffolks mature very early and can do light work at 2 years old, with full work at 3. Their working life lasts well into their 20s.

The Suffolk is known for being easy to train, being also docile and hardworking. It is capable of almost any kind of work and is easy to maintain. Coats are various shades of chestnut. Height is 16.1–17.1hh.

SUMBA (Indonesia)

The Sumba is primitive in appearance, and with its dorsal stripe and dark points is not dissimilar to Mongolian and Chinese natives that were probably descendants of the Asian Wild Horse. In their native Indonesia, Sumbas are ridden by small boys in competitions of equestrian dancing, with jingling bells attached to the horses' knees.

These ponies are not without their charm, with largish but rather pretty heads. They have small, black-tipped ears, slightly dished noses, and large attractive almond-shaped eyes which are soft and expressive. The neck is rather short, with a compact straight-backed body. The quarters are also small, and the shoulders straight. The legs are long and rather fine. There is a black dorsal stripe from poll to tail, an indication of its primitive heritage.

Sumbas are kind and willing. They are tough and hardy with good stamina and make good children's ponies.

They are usually dun, with dark points, and their height is around 12hh.

The Sumba's dun colour and dorsal stripe indicate that not much progress has been made in evolving from its primitive state.

SWEDISH WARMBLOOD
(Sweden)

Like many European warmbloods, the Swedish Warmblood was developed to produce a supreme cavalry horse, endowed with strength, stamina, intelligence and courage.

In the 17th century the Royal Stud at Flyinge mated indigenous coldblooded stock with many European breeds, most specifically Iberian, Friesian, Barb and Arab. This produced the breed's foundation stock and a Swedish Warmblood stud book was eventually opened in 1874.

Before they could be registered, it was necessary not only for horses to undergo stringent tests to ensure that their conformation was up to standard, but that action, stamina, temperament and performance should also be rigorously tested.

Over the next 100 years or so, the breed was refined and improved with infusions of Hanoverian, Trakehner, English Thoroughbred and more Arab. Consequently it could almost be said that the quality warmblood we know today was especially designed for the purpose, that is, to excel at competition; this includes dressage, eventing, showjumping and carriage-driving.

The head is rather fine and long, with a straight nose and a well-defined

muzzle with flared nostrils. The ears are long, giving an impression of alertness, and the eyes are bright and intelligent. The neck is long and elegant with a well-developed crest. The shoulders are muscular and sloping with a good broad chest and a deep girth. The back is medium-length with strong loins and well-developed quarters. The long legs are muscular with large joints, and the hooves are strong and shapely.

These horses are respected for their jumping ability and excellent paces. They are willing, obedient and intelligent and have a lively and spirited demeanour.

The coat comes in all solid colours. Height is usually 16.1–17hh, though some are smaller.

Bred to be a cavalry horse, the Swedish Warmblood is now a quality competition horse.

SWISS WARMBLOOD
(Switzerland)

The Swiss Warmblood is based on Switzerland's highly respected Einsiedler breed, which dates back at least to the 11th century; in fact, there is evidence that Benedictine monks in Einsiedeln were breeding the horses as early as 1064.

For many centuries the Einsiedler, which is a strong and athletic animal, was used as a riding and driving horse. Gradually the breed was enhanced when Norman and Hackney blood

BELOW LEFT: These two Einsiedlers are being ridden by soldiers of the Swiss Army. The Einsiedler was remodelled to produce the Swiss Warmblood.

OPPOSITE: The Swiss Warmblood is a quality horse with excellent conformation. It has many successes in international competition, particularly in the disciplines of showjumping and dressage.

were added, and infusions of Anglo-Norman bloodlines were also introduced at a later date.

But it was in the 20th century that the breed really took off; Selle Français and Anglo-Arab were then added, making the horse much finer and warmblooded. Then, in the 1960s, the Swiss decided they needed their own performance and competition horse, so using the remodelled Einsiedler, other European warmbloods, such as Hanoverian, Holstein, Trakehner and Thoroughbred, were used.

The result was the Swiss Warmblood, a high-quality sports horse that excels at dressage, showjumping and carriage-driving competitions. In its early stages, the National Stud at Avenches used imported stallions, but now that the breed has developed its own standard Swiss Warmbloods are used.

The head is of medium size and of a good quality, with a straight or slightly dished nose, intelligent eyes, and alert, medium-length ears. The neck is long and elegant with a slight crest. The body is of medium length, with a good strong, sloping shoulder, a broad chest, and a deep girth. The legs are long and well-developed with well-shaped hooves.

These quality horses are known for their excellent paces and superb jumping ability, having had many successes in international competition. Swiss Warmbloods are kind, willing horses and are relatively easy to train.

Coats come in all solid colours. They stand around 16hh.

TENNESSEE WALKING HORSE (U.S.A.)

The Tennessee (or Plantation) Walking Horse originated in the deep south of the United States and was recognized as the ideal utility breed to transport plantation owners around their large estates. The smooth, gliding gait of the 'Walker' (as the breed is also known) provided hours of comfort in the saddle; the movement is performed from the elbow rather than the shoulder, thus transmitting the minimum of movement to the rider. Although still widely ridden for pleasure, the Walker is nowadays extensively bred for the show ring, and is also used as a general riding and harness horse.

In fact there are two or three characteristic gaits, the flat-footed walk, the running walk, and the canter. The first horse perceived to have this natural talent was foaled in 1837, but it took another 50 years or so to establish the breed as it is today. The Thoroughbred, Standardbred, American Saddlebred, Narragansett Pacer, and Morgan bloodlines, all played their part in establishing this distinctive breed, but it was one stallion, foaled in 1886, that became the foundation stallion, possessing all the qualities such as the delightful

temperament and the characteristic gaits. Nearly all the offspring inherited their sire's traits and he subsequently enjoyed many successful years at stud. Once a breed association became well-established,

approximately 300,000 horses were registered.

The Walker has a large head with a straight profile, gentle eyes, and pointed ears. The neck is arched and muscular, with a broad base which

enables the horse to carry its head high and elegantly. The breed has plenty of bone, which adds to its sturdiness, and has a short-coupled and level topline. The limb joints are well-made, with particularly powerful hocks that allow the hindlegs to step well under the body. The tail is often nicked and set artificially high. The tail hair is usually left long.

Walkers are naturally gentle and calm, but it is their unusual gaits for which they are most famous. Although the gaits are inherited they need to be developed by further training. The flat walk, running walk, and canter are natural to the breed. The running walk has several variations: the rack, the stepping pace, the fox-trot, and single-foot.

Coats come in nearly all colours, but especially black, chestnut, brown, grey, roan or bay. Height is 15–17hh.

The Tennessee Walking Horse is famous for its unusual gaits. It is now used extensively for pleasure and also in the show ring.

TERSKY (Russia)

The Tersky or Tersk is a true
performance horse, specializing in
endurance, racing, jumping and
dressage. Not only has it excellent
sporting and athletic capabilities, but it
is also one of the most beautiful of the
Russian breeds.

Originating in the northern
Caucasus, the breed is now
concentrated at the Stavropol Stud.
Once, breeding and rearing took place
on the steppes, with the result that
weaker stock succumbed to wolves or
died of disease. Survival of the fittest
has consequently made the breed
incredibly tough.

The modern breed is a product of
the early 20th century, based on the
Strelets Arab, which was produced by
crossing Anglo-Arabs with Orlovs, and
developed by crossing Arabs with old-
type Terskys to which Thoroughbred
blood had also been introduced.

There are three variations of
Tersky: the first is lightweight, fine
and Arab-like in appearance, and is
known as the Eastern type. The second

The Tersky is one of Russia's finest breeds. It
has a good deal of Arab and Thoroughbred in its
make-up which greatly enhances its capabilities
in competition.

is a middleweight, and one that is sturdier and longer in the back, with a frame that is thicker-set, while the heavier type has received infusions of Trakehner.

The Tersky is a horse of medium height and great beauty, based on Arabian bloodlines which are reflected in its appearance. The head is finely chiselled with a dished profile. The eyes are large and intelligent, and the nostrils flared.

The Tersky has a wonderful temperament that combines kindness and intelligence with courage and stamina.

The coat colour is predominantly grey, usually with an attractive metallic sheen, but black, chestnut or bay are also possible. Height is 15–16hh.

THOROUGHBRED

The Thoroughbred is probably the most important breed of all and is the best known of all the British breeds. Its history dates to the 17th century, when farmers and landowners in England were becoming increasingly interested in racing. Until that time, local horses, not specifically bred for the purpose, were raced, and it soon became apparent that in the quest for success a selective breeding programme was required. This was all the more pressing when gambling became popular with the public at large.

The wealthier landowners recognized the fact that the native horses had stamina but were lacking speed, so between 1689 and 1729 horses were imported from the Middle East to improve the racing stock. It is generally accepted that the modern Thoroughbred stems from three such stallions: the Byerley Turk, the Darley Arabian, and the Godolphin Arabian, all of which had long careers working at stud. Between them, they established the three bloodlines of Herod, Eclipse and Matchem, which were pivotal to the British Thoroughbred, though the name was not applied to the breed until 1821.

Although initially bred with racing in mind, the qualities of the Thoroughbred make it an ideal horse for all other equestrian disciplines, e.g. eventing, showjumping, dressage, etc. The Thoroughbred has been exported far and wide to improve racing stocks, but has also been used to improve hundreds of other breeds as well.

Thoroughbreds reached the United States in the 1730s – all direct descendants of the three famous foundation stallions – where they were generally similar to those elsewhere; recently, however, a distinctive American type has emerged, with longer hindlegs and a longer stride, making its quarters appear higher by comparison.

The Thoroughbred is a truly beautiful and athletic animal, with long, clean limbs, a fine, silky coat, an elegant profile, and a muscular body. The eyes are always large and intelligent, the ears finely sculpted.

HORSES

Built for toughness, stamina and speed, the Thoroughbred is the ultimate racing machine.

Thoroughbreds are courageous, honest and bold. In fact, one has only to watch a steeplechase or hurdle race to see that this is the case. Often the Thoroughbred is described as 'hot-headed', and while this is probably true of some individuals, which may be more sensitive than others, most are a pleasure to own and ride. All true colours are acceptable, though in recent years palamino and coloured horses have also been developed. Height is 15–17hh.

The Thoroughbred is the king of the horse world, and as a performer is second to none. Its bloodlines have improved many other breeds, particularly the warmbloods.

TRAKEHNER (Germany/Poland)

The Trakehner is the most elegant and most Throughbred-like of all the warmbloods. Nowadays, because of its athleticism and paces, it is predominantly used for competition, particularly dressage and eventing.

The Trakehner's history is a chequered one, dating to 1732 when the first Trakehner stud was founded in East Prussia, now part of Poland but then in Germany. The stud became the main source of stallions for the whole of Prussia and the area quickly became famous for its beautiful and elegant coach horses.

The Trakehner came into being when native horses of the region were bred with Thoroughbreds and Arabs, infusions which gave it both speed and endurance. Within 50 years, however, the emphasis had shifted from producing coach horses to the breeding of chargers for the cavalry, which continued until the Second World War, when the Trakehner stud was completely destroyed. Fortunately, towards the end of the war, about 1,000 horses were saved when they were trekked west with refugees escaping from the Russian invasion. Although some of the horses died on the way, due to the harsh conditions, sufficient survived to continue the breed. Today,

breeding of the Trakehner is again taking place in its place of origin as well as in other countries.

In terms of appearance, the Trakehner resembles the middleweight Thoroughbred. The head is fine with an intelligent and interested expression. The profile is straight and similar to that of the Thoroughbred. The neck and shoulders are shapely, the back short and strong, and the quarters powerful. The legs are strong and straight, producing a powerful and straight action.

The Trakehner has an excellent temperament, being amiable, obedient and courageous. Although resembling the Thoroughbred, it is without the 'hot' temperament associated with that breed. For this reason, breeders looking

The Trakehner has a chequered history, but today is popular as a competition horse, excelling in top dressage and showjumping.

for an infusion of Thoroughbred without this trait often select Trakehner stallions instead.

All solid coat colours are acceptable. Height is 16–16.2hh.

UKRAINIAN SADDLE HORSE
(Ukraine)

This is a relatively modern breed – in fact, only about 50 years old – formed by crossing Hungarian mares (Nonius, Furioso North Star, Gidrán), with Trakehner, Hanoverian and Thoroughbred stallions.

The development of the breed was monitored so closely that an extremely useful warmblood was developed in a relatively short space of time, one that was suitable for all disciplines.

Horses are rigorously performance-tested early in their lives before they are sold on, and only the best are retained for breeding purposes.

Like most warmbloods, the Ukrainian Saddle or Riding Horse has a kind and obliging nature and a positive attitude to work. It is also courageous and bold.

The breed is refined and elegant, its Thoroughbred blood being immediately apparent. The eyes are large and bright and the expression intelligent. The profile is straight.

Coats come in most solid colours, particularly bay, chestnut and black. Height is up to 16.1hh.

In its present form, the Ukrainian Saddle Horse is only around 50 years old. It was bred specifically as a performance warmblood.

VLADIMIR HEAVY DRAFT
(Russia)

The Vladimir originated at the turn of the 20th century in the provinces of Vladimir and Ivanovo to the north-east of Moscow.

Local mares were mated with imported heavy breeds, mainly Clydesdales, but were also crossed with Shire, Cleveland Bay, Suffolk Punch, Ardennais and Percheron. The result is a horse suitable for all kinds of heavy draft work.

The breed was officially recognized in 1946 and from then on only horses which satisfied strict conformation criteria and performance tests were registered.

A horse that matures early, the Vladimir Heavy Draft can be put to work and stud when it is 3 years old.

The horse displays most of the hallmarks of a heavy breed in terms of its physique. The head is quite large, with a straight or convex profile. The neck is well-proportioned and very muscular, and is set on powerful shoulders. The chest is more developed than that of the Clydesdale, and is very broad. The withers are quite pronounced and the back is rather long and sometimes weak. The girth is deep and the quarters are sloping and muscular. Vladimirs have shortish legs which are usually well-feathered.

The breed is remarkable for its proud posture and majestic appearance. Unlike some of the other heavy breeds, its paces are forward-going, making it suitable for pulling troikas. Today, the Vladimir is still used for work on farms and in transportation.

Bay is the most common colour, but some horses can be black or chestnut. The Vladimir stands between 15 and 16.1 hands high.

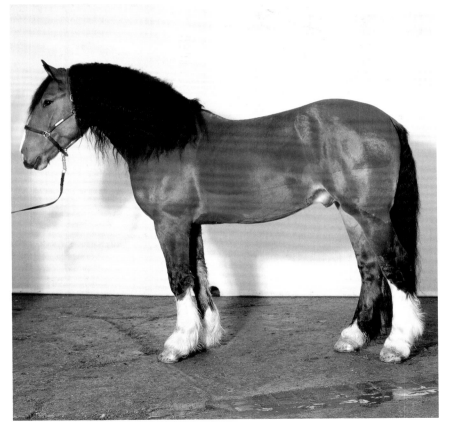

The Vladimir Heavy Draft has all the fine attributes of a heavy horse, with an alert and proud bearing and a lively attitude.

THE WELSH BREEDS (U.K.)

Horses were present in Wales as long as 10,000 years ago. The indigenous breed which inhabited the hills was the Celtic Pony and it is thought that all Welsh breeds known today derive from them.

It is recorded that native stock was being bred in Wales in around 50 BC, when Julius Caesar founded a stud in Merionethshire and was responsible for introducing Arab blood into the breed. The first mention of Welsh Ponies and Cobs were noted in the laws of Hywel Dda, written in AD 930.

RIGHT: The Welsh Pony (Section B) has refined looks combined with strength and toughness. It is an excellent choice for children.

BELOW: The Welsh Mountain Pony (Section A) is the oldest of the Welsh breed.

OPPOSITE: A Welsh (Section B) mare and foal at stud.

Through the centuries, variations of the original wild ponies were developed. Early on in the 20th century, the Welsh Pony and Cob Society

identified four clear types, described below. These are the original, once wild, Welsh Mountain Pony not exceeding 12hh (Section A); the Welsh Pony not exceeding 13hh (Section B); the Welsh Pony of Cob Type up to 13.2hh (Section C); the Welsh Cob of 13.2 –15.2hh (Section D).

WELSH MOUNTAIN PONY
(SECTION A)

The Welsh Mountain Pony is the oldest of all the Welsh breeds. As the name suggests, it is tough, resilient,

sound in limb as well as in constitution. Known for its intelligence, agility, endurance and hardiness, the Welsh Mountain Pony is capable of surviving the harshest of winters. These ponies are now found all over the world and are highly regarded as quality children's riding ponies, and also perform well in harness.

The head is refined, with a small tapering muzzle and small, pricked ears. The eyes are large and bold. These qualities, as well as a dished face, give the Welsh Mountain a distinct resemblance to the Arab which was introduced into the breed. The neck, well-defined withers, and quarters are in proportion to the rest of the pony's body, while the tail is set quite high. The limbs are set square, with well-made joints, and the feet are small, rounded and hard.

This is a pony with great personality and charm, having inherited intelligence and quick-wittedness – traits which the original wild ponies seem to have possessed in abundance. When in action, the gaits must be smooth and the hocks well-flexed.

Coats are mainly grey, but all true colours are acceptable. Ponies should not exceed 12hh.

WELSH PONY (SECTION B)

The Welsh Pony has all the best attributes of the Welsh Mountain Pony, though breeders have accentuated its talents as a riding pony. Moreover, because the Welsh Pony was used for generations on farms for herding sheep, it is also tough and agile.

These qualities, when combined with good looks, jumping ability, and superb conformation for riding, make it perfect as a children's mount.

The Welsh Pony shares many similarities with the Welsh Mountain Pony. The head is refined, with small pricked ears, and the face may be slightly dished. The eyes are large and intelligent. The neck, back and quarters

LEFT: The Welsh Pony (Section C) should resemble a small cob in appearance. It tends to be a little larger than the first two types.

OPPOSITE: The Welsh Cob (Section D) is also very cobby in appearance. It is rather larger than the other three types and is most striking in appearance with extravagant paces. Its size means that it can be ridden by the whole family.

are muscular and in proportion, with the tail set high. The limbs are straight and strong and the hooves strong and rounded.

The Welsh Pony is willing, active and enthusiastic and will always give of its best. They are mainly greys, but all true colours are acceptable. Not to exceed 13.2hh.

WELSH PONY OF COB TYPE (SECTION C)

Originally used for farm work, the Welsh Pony of Cob Type was also used for carting slate from the mines. It is the same height as the Welsh Pony, but sturdier and capable of taking the heavier rider. It was developed more as a harness pony than for ridden work and has a naturally pronounced action, probably inherited from the Hackney, which was introduced into the breed.

The general appearance should be that of a small cob. The eyes are spaced widely apart and the expression is intelligent. Like the other Welsh breeds the ears are small and pricked. The body and legs are sturdier and more cob-like than that of the Welsh Pony, and the feet are also slightly larger. The mane and tail are full.

The Welsh Pony of Cob Type is similar in temperament to the other Welsh breeds, being lively and enthusiastic. It performs well in harness and is also a natural jumper.

All true coat colours are acceptable. For the show ring, however, ponies are preferred with plenty of white on the lower legs. Not to exceed 13.2hh.

WELSH COB (SECTION D)

Of all the Welsh breeds, the Welsh Cob is the most famous. Known for its stunning looks and extravagant paces, it is not only the ultimate working cob, but is also guaranteed to be the centre of attention in the show ring.

The breed dates back to the 11th century, when it was known as the Powys Cob or Powys Rouncy. Welsh Cobs not only possess Welsh Mountain Pony blood, but they were also influenced by imports from all over the Roman Empire. Breeds from Spain, such as the Andalusian, and

the Barb and Arab from North Africa, were all crossed with the early Welsh Cob variety. Later in the 18th and 19th centuries other breeds such as Hackney and Yorkshire Coach Horse were also introduced.

Traditionally, Welsh Cobs were used by the military as well as by farmers; they were so versatile they could be used by anyone needing transport or light haulage.

The Welsh Cob is compact, well-muscled, well-balanced and strong. It has a fine head with large, intelligent eyes and the usual small, pricked ears. The neck is arched and muscular, the back is short-coupled for strength, and the quarters are powerful and rounded. The legs are sturdy and straight and the hooves are in proportion with the animal's body, being hard and rounded.

The Welsh Cob is proud, courageous, and extravagant in action. It is suitable for all disciplines and for all members of the family. All true coat colours are acceptable. Height is 13.2–15.2hh.

WESTPHALIAN (Germany)

Like most European warmbloods, the Westphalian is based on an older, heavier breed which had been native to Westphalia for hundreds of years. This native coldblood was bred with Thoroughbred to produce a warmblood which was first registered as a Westphalian in 1826, when the stud book was opened.

For many years the horse had been used for riding and light carriage work, until the end of the Second World War when measures were taken to improve the breed. Westphalian stock was infused with more Thoroughbred and Arab blood to increase its speed and endurance, as well as intelligence. Hanoverian was also used to ensure good sense and obedience.

The result was a superb quality riding horse which received its true recognition in the 1970s as a competition horse, particularly in showjumping. Nowadays it not only excels at dressage but also eventing.

The head is handsome and broad, with medium wide-apart ears, a straight nose, and clever eyes. The neck is long and well-developed with fairly prominant withers, a straight back, strong loins, and well-muscled quarters. The shoulders are sloping with a broad chest and a deep girth. The legs are well-porportioned and strong with plenty of bone.

The Westaphalian is well-known for its courage and spirit. It is also obedient and easy to handle.

Coats come in all solid colours, and white on the lower legs and head are permitted. Height is 15.2–16.2hh.

The Westphalian is another German success story, bred originally as a carriage and riding horse. It now excels at dressage, eventing and showjumping.

WIELKOPOLSKI (Poland)

The Wielkopolski shares much of its heritage with the Malopolski, which is another breed of Polish Arab, both originally bred as general riding and driving horses also capable of work on farms. Both are based on native Polish Mazuren and Posnan stock, breeds which barely exist now, having become almost totally subsumed into both the Malopolski and Wielkopolski.

The Wielkopolski was established after the Second World War when the native stock, which also contained Konik, was bred with Trakehner, Hanoverian, Thoroughbred and Arab to produce a horse of excellent quality, this being a middleweight used for riding and driving.

There are stringent guidelines to protect the quality of the breed in which all stallions must undergo conformation tests before being allowed to breed.

The Wielkopolski has the Arab wedge-shaped head, though it is somewhat plainer. The nose is straight, with a neat muzzle and large open nostrils. The ears are medium-length and well-shaped and the eyes are lively and intelligent. The neck is high-set, long and elegant, with a slight crest. The shoulders are sloping, with a broad chest and a deep girth. The hindquarters are well-muscled, and the legs are long with good bone and well-shaped hooves.

This is a good all-round competition horse that is also used for driving. It is strong with plenty of stamina and endurance, used on farms and for light draft work in its native land. It has a kind and quiet

Like its close cousin the Malopolski, the Wielkopolski is another Polish Arab type. It is kind and obedient and as useful working on the farm as it is in competition.

temperament and is a willing and obedient worker.

Coats come in all solid colours. Height is 15–16.2hh.

INDEX

INDEX

HORSES